**PRINT CASEBOOKS 7/1987-88 EDITION
THE BEST IN ENVIRONMENTAL GRAPHICS**

*Print
Casebooks 7
1987/1988*

The Best in Environmental Graphics

Written by
Susan Braybrooke

Published by
**RC Publications, Inc.
Bethesda, MD**

Published by RC Publications, Inc.
6400 Goldsboro Road
Bethesda, MD 20817

Manufactured in U.S.A.
First Printing 1986

PRINT CASEBOOKS 7/1987-88 EDITION/THE BEST IN ENVIRONMENTAL GRAPHICS
Library of Congress Catalog Card Number 75-649585
ISBN 0-915734-50-8

PRINT CASEBOOKS 7/1987-88 EDITION
Complete 6-Volume Set
ISBN 0-915734-47-8
3-Volume Set
ISBN 0-915734-55-9

RC PUBLICATIONS
President and Publisher: Howard Cadel
Vice President and Editor: Martin Fox
Creative Director: Andrew P. Kner
Managing Editor: Teresa Reese
Art Director: Charles Hess
Associate Editor: Tom Goss
Graphic Production: Ted Davis

To the continuing discussion of what this *Casebook* is all about—what really constitutes environmental graphics—the 1984 Los Angeles Olympic "look" or environment made a decided contribution. For the duration of the Games, the Jerde Partnership and Sussman/Prejza team succeeded in superimposing another world upon Los Angeles, and in so doing created a veritable "environmental happening," as one juror described it. Everyone agreed that the Olympic graphic event was enormously successful, but it raised some questions that became the theme of this year's jury deliberations.

Because the Olympics lasted for a prescribed amount of time, the "look" was essentially and deliberately temporary in nature. It was fun, it was festive, but it was not intended to go on forever. The predictable Los Angeles summer climate made it possible to create a "paper world." (In fact, it rained three days after the Games ended—so there was an element of luck involved. And anyway, by that time, a lot of the graphic materials had already been stolen as souvenirs.) The whole event was rare and extraordinary, a fiesta that called for elaborate and widespread celebration. But to what extent is this approach relevant to the more humdrum activities of daily life—shopping, for example? And does the very decided trend toward theatricality, exuberance and fantasy, displayed in this year's submissions as a whole, indicate a lack of concern for the more serious information

and communications content of graphic design?

The jurors asked themselves these questions, and made their selections against this background. And they included a high proportion of dash and dazzle, where they felt this was legitimate, called for by the program, and skillfully done. But other schemes were turned down because the signing was too aggressive in inappropriate circumstances, and often because "the typography was very poorly thought out and sloppily applied." In the corporate situation, for example, the signing, they felt, should really be a quiet extension of the architecture. It should tell you what you want to know in a graceful manner; "in a sense," said one juror, "the less you are aware of it as an object, the more successful it is."

All the jurors expressed concern about the generally low standard of typography, although of course there were exceptions, represented by the winning schemes and some others; and they felt that type was often being selected for stylistic reasons . . . because it evoked a certain feeling or atmosphere, but without any real concern for legibility or true understanding of the historical derivation of the effects produced.

Typography, they thought, was certainly getting too little attention in the design schools, and even where it was a mandated course, students were not as interested in it as they should be. "The new freedom to use type in inventive ways," one juror said, "only works if it is based

on a deep knowledge and understanding of the structure and derivation of the different typefaces, although maybe," he went on, "if you really study type, you will find out there are only six typefaces, just as landscape architects who make an exhaustive study of trees find there are only six varieties they can use!"

(Helvetica, incidentally, did not make a very strong showing this year. But not, as in some previous years, because designers seemed to be consciously avoiding it. Perhaps it just did not express the aura they were seeking.)

Of late, apart from such special events as the Olympics and the Louisiana World's Fair, the shopping mall seems to have come in for the most exuberant and virtuoso displays of graphic art. Americans spend lot of time shopping, but what does the American shopper really want from the marketplace? For all the evolving energy that has gone into the design of the retail world, the question still seems to be partly unresolved.

The village square and the small town main street long ago gave way to the shopping mall or plaza—where personal scale and personal service were abandoned in favor of enormous arrangements of goods in large, bland spaces, predictable chain store outlets, convenient parking, and a hot dog if you were lucky. But shoppers, after all, wanted more, or possibly less, than this, and designers began to try to facelift these existing, unlovely places with exterior supergraphics, appealing product signing, and expressions of "love" on the

uniforms of the checkout staff—often, it has to be said, with considerable success.

But now things have gone much further, and the whole experience of shopping has become almost as much of an environmental happening as the Olympics. Greenhouse roofs, banners, awnings, mosaics, and all manner of signs—imposed upon elaborate architectural complexes (often containing some restored, historic structures)—are creating whole new shoppers' worlds in many cities. And in this *Casebook*, two examples on the grand scale, in San Diego and West Los Angeles, are further expressions of the environmental design approach of the Jerde Partnership and Sussman/Prejza Olympic design team. The jury had no doubt about the verve and talent displayed in both these complexes, but they wondered if the activity and drama might be too rich a diet for the everyday shopper, "like being on a continuous high." Might not the suburban housewife prefer to visit a West Side Pavilion, for example, as an occasional "fun" event with friends, and rely on her familiar supermarket-mall for the routine stocking of her shelves and regular replacement of clothes or furniture?

"But even if this is so," asked one juror, "does it really matter? Horton Plaza, for example, is being credited with sparking a revival of San Diego's whole commercial economy." An "event" it may be, but one that has lasting consequences, and may even pep up the local supermarket by association. Benjamin Thompson &

Associates' work at South Street Seaport in New York City hit a very high note in this context. The jury thought the signs were beautiful, very well fabricated, but not an overpowering element in a "legitimately theme-derived retail experience."

Many of the problems discerned in the submissions to this *Casebook* were related, in the jury's view, to architects' continuing tendency to seek graphic consultation too late in the design development process. It was striking how short were the time schedules within which most of the graphics programs presented were completed, and this often accounted for an apparently random placement of building signs, awkward joinery, and dubious legibility. "At least they should consult us when circulation studies are being made," said one juror, "even if they don't call us back for detailed development of the signs until later in the program." In this area, as in many others, it seems, architectural prima-donnaism dies rather hard.

Integration with the environment, something the jurors were always looking out for, was beautifully handled, they thought, in Jan Lorenc's Wildwood Office Park green granite monoliths—but then somewhat disrupted by the enormous white, "front door" sign sculpture introduced later to signify a change in the development of, and architectural approach to, the project. But the jurors were concerned that a number of submitted "environmentally sensitive" signing programs

were ignoring DOT regulations, resulting not only in confusion for users, but in possible liability suits. "I always look for the way the most straightforward, the dumbest sign, if you will, is handled," said one juror, "because this will tell me how carefully the entire scheme was worked out." "Arrows," said someone else, "are also very revealing." And then, predictably, the documentation of the submissions themselves came in for justifiable criticism. While the quality of the photography was unusually high this year, inadequate explanation and illogical slide sequences forced a conscientious jury to try to puzzle out "who did what and why" in far too many cases. This, they felt, was a pity, since the *Print Casebook* awards program "is one of the few to offer more than a 'beauty contest' by providing an opportunity to reward process as well as product." Those submitting their work for consideration should make it easier for the jurors to probe further than skin deep.
—*Susan Braybrooke*

Richard Burns

Richard Burns received a Master of Science degree in visual design from the Institute of Design, Illinois Institute of Technology, and a BA from Indiana University. He began his graphic design career with Unimark International in Chicago. In 1970, he formed Burns Design, and subsequently affiliated with Sasaki Walker Associates as director of design for SWA Communications, the firm's graphics division. In 1974 he founded the GNU Group, Sausalito, California, and continues as the company's president. Burns was instrumental in forming the Society of Environmental Graphics Designers (SEGD), a national professional organization, and serves on its board of directors. He is a frequent lecturer and speaker at universities and seminars throughout the country.

Casebook Jurors

David Gibson   Gary W. Hinsche   John Muhlhausen   Rebecca Rose

David Gibson was a founding partner in 1980 of Two Twelve Associates, a New York graphic design and communications firm where he is responsible for much of the work in environmental graphics, typography, book and publications design. Gibson earned a Master of Fine Arts in graphic design from Yale University in 1980. He did undergraduate studies, from 1969-1973, at Nova Scotia College of Art and Design, and earlier at Cornell University. Gibson served as project design manager for the Ontario Ministry of Natural Resources and graphic designer for Toronto-based Eskind Waddell. More recently, he was graphic designer for Harbor Festival, New York City's 1986 4th of July celebration. He also designed the identity and sign system for Millender Center, a mixed-use development in downtown Detroit. He has designed environmental graphics for the Harlem Urban Development Corporation and the Central Park Administration, and is a member of the Metropolitan Transit Authority's arts advisory committee.

Gary W. Hinsche, a 1968 graduate of California State University, Long Beach, is president of Hinsche + Associates, a full-service marketing and graphic design firm founded in 1976 and based in Santa Monica, California. He bagan his career with the Los Angeles design firm of Robert Miles Runyan & Associates, where he became vice-president and design director. Hinsche has received numerous national and international awards for graphic design excellence in corporate identity and collateral programs, facilities/capabilities brochures, environmental design projects, packaging and other corporate communications programs. In 1986, he was vice-president of the Los Angeles Art Directors Club, and has held staff positions at the Art Center College of Design in Pasadena and at California State University, Long Beach.

President of Muhlhausen Design & Associates, a Roswell, Georgia, design firm specializing in environmental and corporate graphics, John Muhlhausen studied at the College of William and Mary before transferring to the Rhode Island School of Design, where he received a Bachelor of Fine Arts in graphic design in 1963. Since then, Muhlhausen has been associated with architectural, industrial and graphic design offices in the U.S. and Denmark. In 1969, he received international recognition for the development of UniSign Systems, which was perhaps the first modular system for assembling exterior and interior signage. Representing the Society of Environmental Graphics Designers (SEGD), of which he is a board member, he served on a task force to develop national guidelines for airport signing. His book *Wind and Sail* was selected by the American Institute of Graphic Arts as one of the 50 best books of 1972. His work has appeared in Interiors, ID, CA, Graphis and *Print Casebooks*.

After receiving her BFA degree in graphic design from Philadelphia College of Art in 1969, Rebecca Rose worked for the Philadelphia architectural firm of Geddes Brecher Qualls Cunningham as a graphic designer. She moved to New York to work as a graphic designer for Henry Dreyfuss Associates, then as director of graphic design for The Gruzen Partnership. In 1983, Rose began working for Vignelli Associates, where she is vice-president, architectural graphics. She has been instrumental in creating the signing for such architectural projects as, in New York City, the AT&T building, Equitable Tower, the International Design Center, Park Avenue Tower, and 1285 Avenue of the Americas. Other signing projects were for the Cleveland Playhouse, San Francisco's 580 California Street, and 1000 Wilshire in Los Angeles. Also involved in graphic design at Vignelli, Rose worked on the award-winning hardcover development books for Park Tower.

Casebook Writer

Susan Braybrooke

Index

Projects

A writer, editor and public relations consultant in architecture and design, Susan Braybrooke has published articles in a number of professional journals. Her book on the design of research laboratories, *Design for Research,* for which she received funding from the National Endowment for the Arts, was published in early 1986 by John Wiley. Also published by Wiley were two books that she edited—*AIA Metric Building and Construction Guide,* appearing in 1980, and *Architecture: The Design Experience,* by Hugh Stubbins (1976). She was the author of *Casebooks 3, 4, 5, and 6/The Best in Environmental Graphics.*

Clients/Sponsoring Organizations

Allied Chemical Corp. **74**
Apple Computer, Inc. **22, 25**
Boylston Associates **20**
Charles Center/Inner Harbor Management Corp. **74**
Continental Insurance **17**
Cornerstone Development Co. **60**
East Bank Riverfront Partners **31**
Gensler and Associates/Architects **83**
Hahn, Ernest W., Inc. **47**
Holland America Line USA, Inc. **40**
Holland Amerika Lijn, The Netherlands **40**
Leone, Giovanni and Janette **38**
Los Angeles Olympic Organizing Committee (LAOOC) **64, 69, 72**
Louisiana World Exposition **86**
Mahoney-Sewell Associates **35**
Modular Architecture, Inc. **77**
Port Authority of New York and New Jersey, Aviation Dept. **44**
Rockefeller Group, The **54**
Rouse Co., The **10**
Sunset Group, The **80**
Texaco Refining and Marketing, Inc. **14**
Trammel Crow Co. **94**
U.S. Fidelity and Guarantee Co. **91**
Westfield, Inc. **51**
Wildwood Office Park **28**

Designers/Architects/Consultants

Aasland, Marie **44**
Alexander, Dean **40**
Anspach Grossman Portugal, Inc. **14**
Apple Computer Creative Services **22, 25**
Ashley, Roy, & Associates **28**
Ayers, Will **14**
Benit, Wynne **40**
Berman, Jerry **35**
Brandon, Kelly **60**
Bricker, John **83**
Bright & Associates **40**
Bright, Keith **40**
Bush, Charles **25**
Cameron, Lindy **25**
Childs, Bertman, Tseckares & Casendino **20**
Communication Arts, Inc. **86**
Cooper Carry & Associates, Architects **28**
Cuyler, Scott **72**
Cvek, Sava **20**
Daddino, Paul **25**
D'Agostino, Bruce **10**
Debrito, Vincent **40**
Design/Joe Sonderman, Inc. **57**
Diaz-Azcuy, Orlando **83**
D.I. Design & Development Consultants, Inc. **31**
Dudrow, Ann **91**
Emerson, Karen **35**
Engineering and Inspection Systems **28**
Eskew, R. Allen **86**
Eubanks, Victoria **38**
Fagan, Mark **10**
Felperin, Peter **14**
Felton, Richard **14**
Ferris, James **25**
Foy, Richard **86**
Franzman Davis & Associates **28**
Gemmell, Rob **22**
Gensler Graphics Group **83**
Gericke, Michael **86**
Gibbs Landscaping Co. **28**
Gordon, Gail **83**
Gorman, Robert **74**
Guard, John **40**
Guerard, James **69, 72, 80**
Gutow, Deborah **54**
Hanegraaf, Cynthia L. **74**
Harsh, Ronn **22**
Head, Mary **57**
Hennes, Cathy **40**

Higgs, Roy **31**
Hinsche & Associates **69, 72, 80**
Hinsche, Gary **69, 72, 80**
Hoover, Donna **86**
ISD **91**
Izzo, Chuck **10**
Jarriel, J. Brett **28**
Jerde, Jon **64**
Jerde Partnership, The **47, 51, 64, 69, 72**
Jones, Carole **60**
Kan, Chi-ming **86**
Kelly, James **10**
Kiel, Donald L. **17**
Kinzig, Susie **86**
Klein, Kurt **40**
Klein, Larry **40, 64, 69, 72**
Kline, Donald **14**
Koch, Mark **60**
Korsunsky Krank Erickson **31**
Kudrycki, Tamara **38**
Land Design/Research, Inc. **74**
Landkamer, Mark **40**
Lee, Adrian **77**
Light, Todd **17**
Loheed, Philip **10**
Lopez, Elsa **77**
Lopez, Maria **77**
Lorenc, Jan **28**
Lorenc, Jan, Design, Inc. **28**
Love, Kenneth **14**
Marshall, Mike **60**
Meckell, David **64**
Miller, Hanson Westerbeck Bell Architects, Inc. **31**
Mills, Michael **40**
Miner, Peter **10**
Modular Architecture, Inc. **77**
Mok, Clement **25**
Montgomery Design **77**
Montgomery, Margaret **77**
Moore, Charles **86**
Morgan and Associates **38**
Mullaly, Patrick **74**
Murray, Pat **69, 72**
O'Malley & Co. Ltd. **94**
Palaia-Svedburg **31**
Parkhurst, Ken **40**
Pereira, William L., Associates **35**
Perez Associates **86**
Peters, Richard **86**
Petrie, Daphne **10**
Pillorgé, Nicole **91**
Pirtle Design **94**

Pirtle, Woody **94**
Poore, Suzi **40**
Port Authority of New York and New Jersey, Engineering Dept. **44**
Prejza, Paul **64**
Promen, Timothy **74**
Public Access Systems **54**
Quirk, Tom **10**
Raynes, Coco **20**
Raynes, Coco/Graphics, Inc. **20**
Reilly, Joan **10**
Reynolds, Smith & Hills **40**
Roe, William **10**
Romano, Ellen **25**
RTKL Associates, Inc. **91**
Sargent, Peter **40**
Schroeder, Mike **94**
Shank, John **10**
Sidjakov Berman & Gomez **35**
Sign Co., The **10**
Silverstein, Erik **54**
Siodmark, Geoff **40**
Slatter, Gail **38**
Smith, Jim **54**
Stein, Ellie **77**
Suiter, Tom **22**
Sussman, Deborah **64**
Sussman/Prejza **47, 51, 64, 69, 72**
Swanke Hayden Connell Architects **17**
Taguchi, Yasuhiko **57**
Thompson, Benjamin **10**
Thompson, Benjamin, & Associates **10**
Tom, John **69, 72, 80**
TRA Architecture Engineering Planning Interiors **60**
TRA Graphic Design **60**
Turnbull, William **86**
VanHook, Patrick **86**
Vicente, José **77**
Vick, Barbara **35**
Walker, Jo **40**
Wander, Sheldon D. **44**
Weber, Christina **38**
Weber Design **38**
Whitebay, Diane **44**
Wiethman, Jeff **94**
Wood, Raymond **40**
Woods, Paul **25**
Yoshimi, Toshi **83**
Zuidweg, Lawrence **40**

South Street Seaport

The opening up and revitalization of New York City's long-neglected waterfront is nowhere more evident than at bustling, vibrant South Street Seaport. Where just a few years ago were crude fishmarkets, unadorned clam bars, a small museum and one or two tall ships riding at anchor, there are now restaurants, pubs, boutiques, yachts, an array of elegant and attractive merchandise, and indoor and outdoor cafés serving seafood in every form, from oysters Rockefeller to fish and chips.

The task of identifying the disparate elements within a unified and expressive graphic theme fell to Benjamin Thompson and Associates, architects for the Fulton Market and Pier 17 Pavilion buildings, and well-known for their distinguished work in other such ventures, particularly Boston's Faneuil Hall (see *Environmental Graphics Casebook 4,* pages 31-33).

At South Street Seaport, their graphic assignment was wide-ranging, covering overall identification of the South Street Seaport Museum, logos for the two new buildings—Fulton Market and Pier 17—and signs for some interior public spaces, as well as for the individual shops and stalls of some 200 tenants. While BTA designed the project logo and building signs themselves, in the interests of variety they allowed individual vendors to execute the tenant signing—within pre-established design and materials guidelines. Their goal was to create a system that would help people to find their way around quickly and

easily, but without being hit over the head by the graphics. "The signing is there for those who need or want it," says Jane Thompson," without being so assertive as to become the dominant design feature. By using clean and dignified lettering—Times Roman and Bodoni—and exposed fasteners, standard angles and metal panels, we feel we responded to the nature of the buildings, which were designed with exposed steel frames and other 'industrial' details. This rather reserved and dignified approach was meant to help provide a background against which individual tenants would create a more flamboyant and idiosyncratic counterpoint."

Integration of graphics and architecture was important, as was the selection of a design and materials vocabulary that would somehow express the history and essence of the place. The logo for Fulton Market is hand-carved in granite slabs that combine to form a wall cap encompassing the building and marking each important opening and pediment. A single display of cutout metal letters with a white enamel finish marks the principal corner at Fulton Street, and harmonizes with the metal canopy from which it hangs. The Pier 17 Pavilion is lettered on its two sides and there is a proposal to place an elevated sign in Helvetica along its ridgepole. The scale makes the signs clearly visible from the Brooklyn shoreline and from passing boats, rather in the manner of 19th-century rail terminal piers.

The Bluefish, which is the Seaport logo, is rendered in

1.

2.

3.

4.

1. Pier 17 sign is scaled for legibility from the Brooklyn shore and from boat traffic.
2. Opening ceremonies for the Pier 17 building were held in September 1985.
3. Site directory is topped by bluefish logo.
4. Changeable area shop directory maintains overall vocabulary of white lettering on darker background.
5. Site plan for multi-block South Street Seaport area.

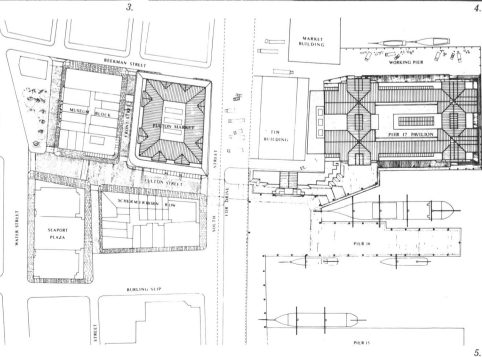

5.

various materials to become the theme for directories, building signs and illuminated signs in both buildings.

The materials palette was specified to respond to the industrial/market esthetic of the buildings and recall the metal, porcelain and painted signs indigenous to the history of the area.

Painted metal letters, either cut from, or applied to, painted metal panels, were bolted to a variety of frame types constructed of steel angles, channels and pipes. Specialty signs include neon shapes on silkscreened plexiglass, bronze and acrylic castings, and carved granite. Green, which has historic connections with traditional market signing, is used in a range of shades. Lettering is primarily white on a dark background, although in some places black letters appear on a white background with a colored border. The only major fabrication problem revolved around difficulties in getting delivery of porcelain enamel panels on a workable schedule. In the end, a durapox enamel finish was used instead.

As master planners for the entire Seaport Museum development and architects for two buildings, BTA was able to develop, refine and coordinate the graphics program along with the evolution of the architecture.

6.

7.

9.

10.

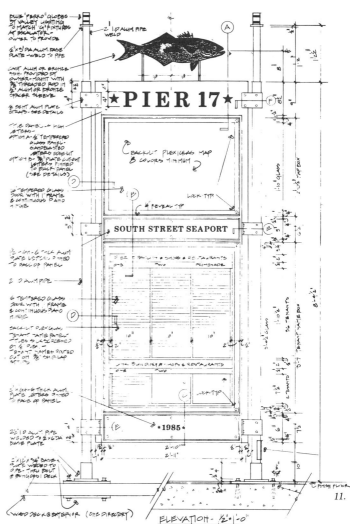

11.

12.

6. Overscale lettering is as effective from close up as from a distance.
7. Drawing showing proposed Seaport sign on ridgepole of Pier 17 building. Approval has been given by Landmarks Commission but was still pending at press time from Zoning Board.
8. Cutout white enameled metal letters hang from a metal canopy in the best traditions of market signing.
9. Special neon treatment of bluefish logo.
10. Building name sign hung at main entry is in the spirit of "industrial" architecture.
11. Working drawing of project directory.
12. Tenant signing is festive yet restrained, following guidelines laid down by the architects.

Client: The Rouse Co., Columbia, MD
Design firm: Benjamin Thompson & Associates, Cambridge, MA
Designers: Tom Quirk, Joan Reilly, Chuck Izzo
Architect: Benjamin Thompson & Associates: Benjamin Thompson, principal; Bruce D'Agostino and Philip Loheed, partners-in-charge; John Shank, Charles Izzo, project architects; Tom Quirk, project architect/construction; Daphne Petrie, Peter Miner, Joan Reilly, Mark Fagan, William Roe, project team
Fabricators: Letterama, Inc. (James Calderone); Persson Co.
Consultant: James Kelly, The Sign Co.

Texaco Service Stations

The gas station is as American and ubiquitous as apple pie, and its evolution is a good indication of the pulse of life in the American heartland. The gas stations of the past seem now to be quite touching reminders of their eras, which they expressed through some degree of standardization. And, indeed, it is just this standardization that makes them so familiar, so recognizable, so inevitable a feature of almost any landscape.

Since it is so broadly applied, the image of the gas station becomes crucial to an oil company's success at the pumps. Recognizing this, Texaco hired the New York marketing communications and design firm of Anspach Grossman Portugal to develop for them a whole new retail presentation. Charged with this comprehensive challenge and mission, the design team, headed by Kenneth Love, conducted a survey of Texaco customers in a number of locations, and found that, while the visual image of the buildings and signing had a strong impact, the services and products provided and the manner in which they were presented were equally important. So the design program had to concern itself with the integration and identification of the different elements—full-service pumps, self-service pumps; service centers, food marts, restrooms, car wash uniforms, oil cans—beneath the overall umbrella of the canopy unit.

Independent user research had established that Texaco had made a mistake in the 1960s by down-playing the well-known lone star logo and placing it within a hexagon bearing the company's name. So AGP brought back the star; developed a sophisticated but striking color palette of white and red on black and two shades of gray; used various weights of Helvetica to advantage, and rearranged the architectural elements to create a more "aggressive and consistent package." They also upgraded the lighting to give added impact to the design.

After design drawings and scale models were approved, a prototype was built by a North Carolina manufacturer, Beaman Corporation, who now manufactures the modules—canopy unit, car wash, food mart, and so on, on an assembly line, and then ships them for setting up at the site as a total package. The package imagery was helpful in selling the whole program to the client, who was asked to think of the "gas station as a package, but one that's too big to put on a shelf; the shelf in this case being the street or highway."

All the components of the redesign package were included in a detailed graphic standards manual prepared by AGP to guide future installations. An independent post-design study by Crosley Research indicated a favorable public response to colors, messages and overall presentation. The *Casebook* jurors, wondering if this much-heralded program was really as good as it was cracked up to be, ultimately decided that it was.

1.

2.

Client: Texaco Refining and Marketing Inc., Houston
Design firm: Anspach Grossman Portugal, Inc., New York City
Designers: Kenneth Love, design director; Peter Felperin, senior industrial designer; Richard Felton, senior graphic designer; Donald Kline, senior graphic designer; Will Ayres, senior package designer
Fabricator: Beaman Corp.

1. *Color palette of white, red, black and two tones of gray creates a striking integration of signing, equipment and architecture.*
2. *Industrial hardware is an effective sign-organizing device.*
3. *Evolution of the famous lone star logo.*
4. *Carefully integrated lighting dramatizes the gas station that is more than a gas station.*

Evolution of a Symbol

	1903
	1907
	1909
	1915
	1936
	1963
	1982

3.

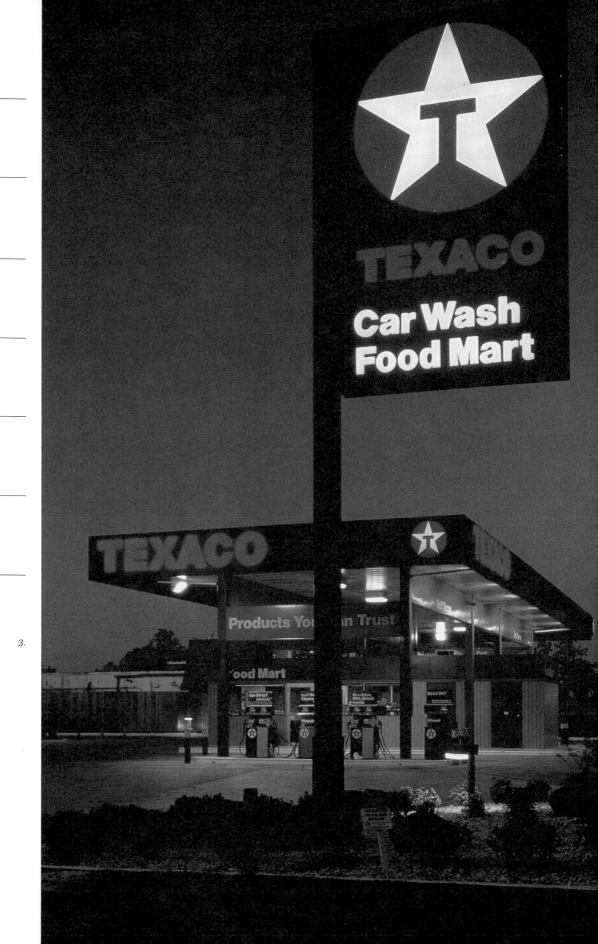

4.

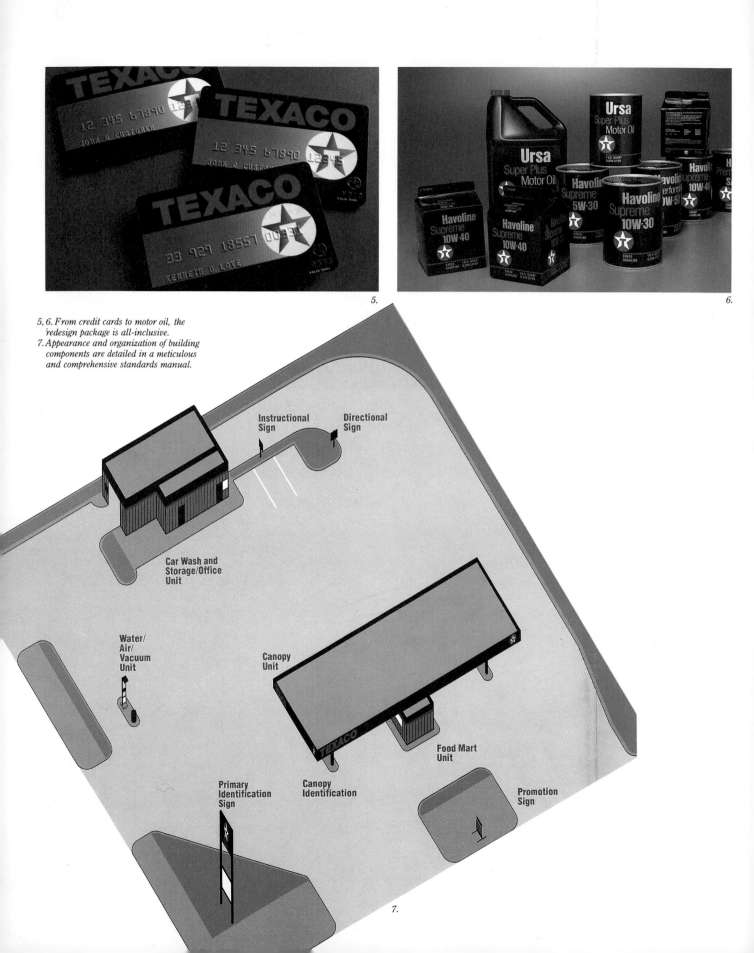

5, 6. From credit cards to motor oil, the
    redesign package is all-inclusive.
7. Appearance and organization of building
    components are detailed in a meticulous
    and comprehensive standards manual.

5.

6.

Instructional
Sign

Directional
Sign

Car Wash and
Storage/Office
Unit

Water/
Air/
Vacuum
Unit

Canopy
Unit

Food Mart
Unit

Primary
Identification
Sign

Canopy
Identification

Promotion
Sign

7.

Continental Center
Construction Tunnel

The only one of the *Casebook* submissions to elicit spontaneous but approving laughter from the jurors, the yellow-cab mural adorning the end wall of a temporary building entrance tunnel clearly succeeded in its objective. By its lighthearted display of concern for the employees, the mural and the tire tracks leading up to it did much to ameliorate an awkward situation, and prevent a pervasive feeling of dissatisfaction from souring the first weeks in a new corporate headquarters.

The Continental Insurance Company's new headquarters on Maiden Lane in New York City had undergone numerous construction delays and move-in postponements. And when the building was finally ready for occupancy, employees still had to use a temporary entrance for several months while the main

lobby was being completed. Employee access to the building was via a temporary construction tunnel built through a back entrance extending 70', making a 90-degree turn and then extending another 70' to the elevators.

To make this inconvenience as palatable as possible, Continental's executives asked their architects, Swanke Hayden Connell, to find an upbeat way to direct people away from the construction areas and down the tunnel to the elevators.

Two bright red, 4' plywood arrows were bolted into the concrete slab at the two main building entrances on Maiden Lane to steer employees round to the back entrance and into the tunnel. Once inside the tunnel, people could follow tire tracks spray-painted (via a hand-cut stencil) onto the carpet, terminating at an 8'-

square wall by the elevators. On this wall, the slightly larger-than-life hand-tinted photostat of a Checker cab makes a dramatic and witty statement.

The original photo of the cab was shot at a street intersection only 200' from Continental Center and in direct alignment with the tunnel path. This touch, once recognized, was especially appreciated by employees using the tunnel.

With a combined design and construction budget of some $18,000, and only four weeks to do the job, designer Donald Kiel first had to have the tunnel walls sandbagged and the tunnel itself pumped out, as heavy rain had caused extensive flooding. Once the concrete floor had dried, it was finished and carpeted, and the walls and ceiling painted. One wall was painted taxicab yellow, so that the cheerful ambience was evident as soon as anyone

entered the tunnel. Because the flooding had damaged the sheetrock tunnel walls, a 3″ black vinyl base was installed all the way along. Optima Regular and Bold were chosen for the applied vinyl lettering on the arrows to be consistent with Continental's corporate identity.

After studying the street-level building plan and making a site visit, Donald Kiel prepared a 30″-by-42″ presentation board of his concept to show to the company's executives and the architectural team. He received their immediate approval, but still had to coordinate the work of six vendors in short order to meet the very stringent deadline. But the results were worth the effort. Employees used the temporary entrance in good spirits for some four months, and the arrows had an unforeseen second function— lunch tables for the construction crews!

1.

2.

1, 2. Plywood arrow bolted into concrete slab (Fig. 1) directs employees to temporary entrance tunnel (Fig. 2).

Client: Continental Insurance, New York City
Design firm: Swanke Hayden Connell Architects, New York City
Designers: Donald L. Kiel, Todd Light
Architects: Swanke Hayden Connell
Fabricator: Chas. E. Maier, Inc.

3. *Tunnel runs 70', makes a sharp turn, then runs another 70' to culminate at elevator banks.*
4, 5. *Tire tracks sprayed on the carpet lead employees to the yellow cab mural.*
6. *Mural photo was shot at nearby street intersection exactly on line with the tunnel's path.*

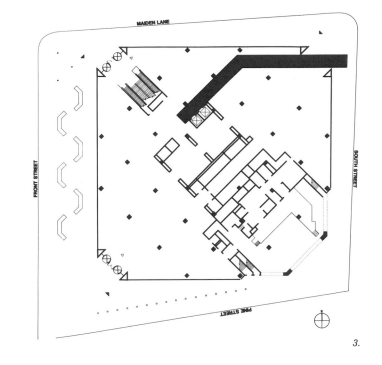

3.

4.

5.

6.

19/Environmental Graphics

399 Boylston Street

A design solution that still merits the now controversial designation, "Less is more," this building identification component of a wider signing program won the *Casebook* jury's approval for an excellent marriage of design and technology in which boldness and transparency combine to create great drama. Since the program demanded that the logo be treated as an extension of the architecture, designer Coco Raynes decided that cast acrylic numerals mounted directly on the glass building facade would "respect perfectly the transparency of the facade and add to the glass reflections."

The concept was very simple, and most of the fine-tuning concerned experiments with the size and type-style of the numerals and refinements of the mounting technique.

The numerals, derived from Futura Light, are 3′7″ high and ⅝″ thick. They were fitted into precisely positioned mounting holes incorporated in the glass panels when they were manufactured. This attachment detail was the main difficulty in the apparently simple solution, since the weight of the numerals and the fact that the glass had to be manufactured with the mounting holes already in position demanded perfect precision and eliminated any possibility of improvisation if the specified solution did not work.

The feasibility of increasing the weight of the acrylic to allow the use of larger and stronger fastening screws was considered but rejected because it would only have increased the stress on the glass.

Much depended on finding a manufacturer willing to go along and take the risk. In the event, the addition of neoprene spacing sleeves between the stainless steel screws, of nylon rings under the screw heads, and of acrylic washers to isolate the numerals from the glass, solved the problems, and the installation worked perfectly. Coco Raynes found considerable challenge and satisfaction in "the extreme precision required, living

dangerously and being right in the end."

One cost benefit of the solution was that it eliminated any need for separate sign lighting. In the daytime, the curves of the numerals are intensified by reflections of natural light; at night, the numbers are strongly defined against the illuminated lobby.

Client: Boylston Associates, Boston
Design firm: Coco Raynes/Graphics, Inc., Cambridge, MA
Designers: Coco Raynes, Sava Cvek
Architect: Childs, Bertman, Tseckares & Casendino, Boston
Fabricators: Karas & Karas Glass Co. (glass); Future Plastics (acrylic); General Sign Co. (installation)

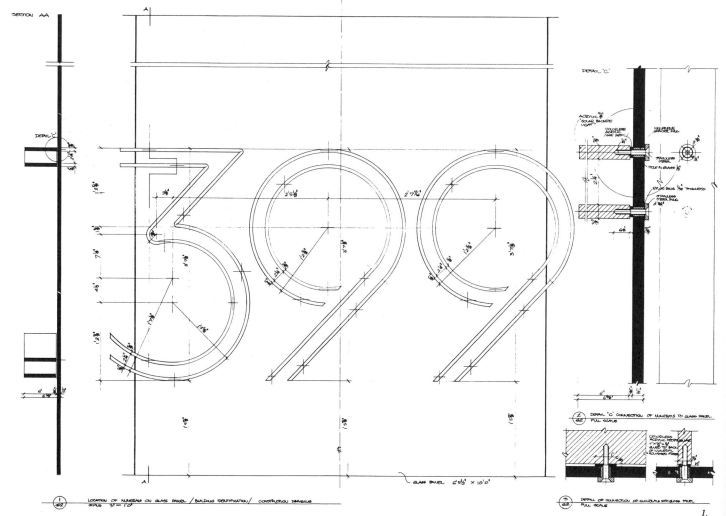

2.

3.

4.

1. Working drawing shows 3'7"-high cast
   acrylic numerals against glass panels with
   pre-manufactured mounting holes.
   Attachment detail was a major challenge
   and required neoprene spacing sleeves,
   and acrylic washers between numerals
   and glass.
2-4. Solution relies on reflectivity and
   transparency to effect a perfect marriage of
   signing and architecture.

Apple Computer

According to the Apple Creative Services Department, "the personal computer industry is an extremely fast-paced and explosive-growth business environment; nothing in real life can really compare to the changes that occur day-to-day here. At Apple there are only three time zones—Real time; Industry time; and Apple time."

This distinction between the computer world and reality is interesting, coming as it does from inside the "big apple" itself. For in a way, this other-worldly quality, this "star wars" aura, if you will, is one of the problems the uninitiated have in trying to relate to computers. We know they virtually run our lives, and yet we can't understand how they work. We know they're "user friendly," but some of us are intimidated by them. We know they are the wave of the future, but somehow we can't drag our feet out of the past.

There is a dichotomy here. The excitement, the pace, the "unreality," are part of the mystique, which the industry apparently wants to keep alive, even while making its products accessible and appealing to an ever-widening hierarchy of user groups.

1-3. Apple's new corporate identity manual, detailing application of the new "white" look to printed media, sparked an expansion of the program to cover corporate and vehicular signing.

4,5. New signing applied to fleet of vehicles shows effective use of the striped apple logo in a large white field.

6. Example of vehicle signing before the new white look.

1.

2.

3.

Apple Corporate Signing

Usually a corporate identity manual follows the invention of a new corporate image and logo as a tool to ensure its correct application in a whole range of locations and circumstances. But in Apple's case, part of the order was reversed. The Creative Services Group were at work on an ID Manual for their new "white look," when they realized that new corporate signing was needed. So in a very real sense, they created their own assignment.

Using their own guidelines, and the new "white look," already being applied to printed media and advertisements, they translated this new approach to vehicular and building signing. The result is a rather streamlined identity, particularly striking, the *Casebook* jury thought, in large-scale application to trailer trucks.

In the building context, white monolithic signs, 45"-, 30"- and 15"-square, carrying the vinyl logo, are fabricated from extruded aluminum, and mounted on horizontal, 15"-high rectangular bases or "blades." (The small signs are mounted on 30"-high vertical blades.) The blades carry the corporate standard type, ITC Garamond Book Condensed to 80 per cent of roman, in PMS 423 gray. The square-sign format works well, as it allows the required area of white field all around Robert Janoff's familiar rainbow-striped apple.

Any problems encountered in getting quality fabrication were resolved, say the designers, as soon as the contractors really understood what was wanted. A post-design survey conducted among vendors and users found

4.

that the type on the vertical blades for the small signs was difficult to read. By changing it to a darker gray, PMS 424, this problem, too, was solved.

5.

Client: Apple Computer, Inc., Cupertino, CA
Design firm: Apple Computer, Inc., Creative Services, Cupertino
Designers: Ronn Harsh, designer; Rob Gemmell, art director; Tom Suiter, creative director
Fabricator: Street Graphics

6.

7, 8. Square aluminum building
identification signs are mounted on
rectangular bases or "blades" to which the
corporate type is applied.
9. Blueprints for signing system.
10. Installation detail—before application of
graphics.

'Pride in Performance' Sales Meeting

Some 1200 fledgling and seasoned sales personnel attending the 1985 international sales meeting at the Hilton Hawaiian Village Hotel in Honolulu found themselves deluged by a colorful bombardment of banners, posters, signs, nametags, canvas bags, and much, much more—all designed by Apple's Creative Services Group in upbeat celebration of a "phenomenal year."

Given a mandate to "make it great! make it different and exciting! make it look like we own the hotel!," the Creative Services Group set about doing just that. They invented a theme graphic based on a somewhat Matisse-inspired figure wearing an oversized medal. Then, using a color palette of PMS yellow, blue, red, green, teal, pink (more or less the colors of the famous striped apple), and adding some Hawaiian-based themes as well, they put their signature on everything.

With only six to eight weeks to complete the assignment, and the need to produce an enormously varied menu in quantities of upwards of 1200, the task was tremendous. It involved teamwork among designers, illustrators and fabricators to achieve design consistency in all graphically-oriented items presented at the meeting. These ranged from luggage-tag to presentation slide; from product exhibit to set design; from multi-media presentation for the awards banquet to customized Hawaiian shirt; or even, it seems, a Marshmallow Man costume, three Ghostbuster uniforms, and a laser-optic fiber Apple logo in the swimming pool.

There were no post-design studies, but, according to art director Clement Mok, these were neither necessary nor possible, because, "with the exception of the giant banners (30′ square and 10′ by 40′), all signage, and I mean all signage, was swiped by the sales force as souvenirs or mementos." This is the kind of user comment that speaks for itself!

Client: Apple Computer, Inc., Cupertino, CA
Design firm: Apple Creative Services, Cupertino
Designers: James Ferris, creative director; Clement Mok, art director; Rob Gemmell, 3D designer; Paul Daddino, exhibit designer; Paul Woods, graphic designer/illustrator; Ellen Romano, graphic designer; Lindy Cameron, graphic designer/illustrator
Fabricators: Emerson Flags, banners; McGibbons, silkscreen posters; Pier 5 Model Shop, exhibit stations; Chart Masters, speaker support; Braverman Production, video modules; ImageStream, video modules, multi-media presentations; Theatre Techniques, staging crew

1.

1. Poster announces theme of 1985 sales meeting in Hawaii.
2. Illustration from welcoming booklet gives details of travel, accommodations and program.

2.

3.

4.

5.

6.

*3, 4. Giant banners keep conference theme
constantly in view.*
*5, 6. Ghostbuster suits and other high-jinx
introduce the new Macintosh Office with a
bang.*
*7, 8. Name tags and Hawaiian shirts were
all part of the graphics program.*
*9. Colorful banners identify the myriad
activities and resources of the conference.*

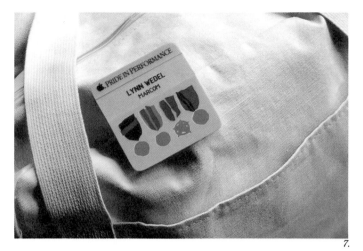

7.

8.

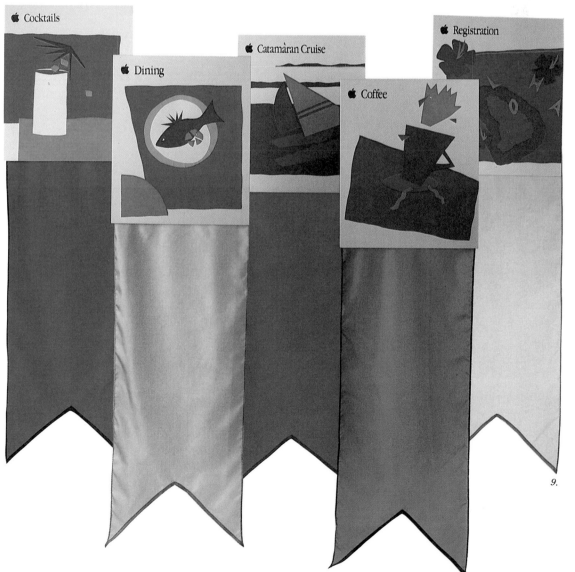

9.

Wildwood Office Park

Integration with the environment was the original theme of both the architecture and the signing program for this 269-acre corporate environment adjoining the Chattahoochee National Park near Atlanta. The architecture was to work with the topography of the land, leaving the deep draws and ridges in their natural condition, and siting buildings were to disappear as far as possible into their environment.

In sympathy with this general philosophy of respect for the land, the design firm of Jan Lorenc Design studied the site with a view to producing "landmark" signs that would be "subdued, controlled, quiet," and yet in some way dynamic. A sculptural solution seemed the only way to go, and so the team evolved a series of green Vermont granite monoliths to carry the Wildwood logo, or individual building identification, and a faceted, organic, sculptural motif carved into the granite. It was this that caught the attention of the *Casebook* jury, who felt that these granite signs were strong symbols of identification "almost perfectly in tune" with their environment. Pairs of monoliths, each one 8′ high by 6′ wide by 1′ deep, are used to mark important site entrances; smaller monoliths, 4′10″ high by 6′10″ wide by 9″ deep, identify the component corporate complexes within the park.

Later, a pair of 28′-high sculptural monoliths, finished in glossy white polyurethane paint, were developed for the primary entrance or "front door" to the park. This was in response to a change in

1.

TYPOGRAPHY ROUTED OUT OF SIGN FACE & INFILLED WITH ⅛″ GREEN ACRYLIC (FLUSH WITH OUTER SURFACE)

1′-3″ (TYP)

1′-2″

4′-10″

WILDWOOD

2.

development policy toward a denser, more urban-scale approach to the architecture.

Jan Lorenc was also responsible for directional and regulatory site signing and some interior and project marketing signs. Most of the aluminum traffic signs have dark-green-painted hardware to harmonize with the natural setting.

Two weights of Meridien type (54 and 54 Bold) were used throughout the system, except where corporate logos were required, "to communicate a chiseled sense of permanence."

1. *Sympathy with grand scenery inspired the signing system.*
2. *Working drawing shows incorporation of lettering in granite monoliths.*
3. *Green granite monoliths mark site entrances and enhance the landscape.*

3.

Client: Wildwood Office Park, a Development of IBM and Cousins Properties, Inc., Marietta, GA (John W. Shern, senior vice-president)
Design firm: Jan Lorenc Design, Inc., Atlanta
Designers: Jan Lorenc, principal-in-charge of design; J. Brett Jarriel, project designer
Architect: Cooper Carry & Associates, Architects
Consultants: Franzman Davis & Associates (land and master planning), Gibbs Landscaping Co. (landscape design/contractors), Roy Ashley & Associates (landscape design), Engineering and Inspection Systems (consulting engineers)
Fabricators: Cold Spring Granite Co. (granite); Concept Unlimited (regulatory and streetscape signs); Design South Signage Div. (primary project landmark sign and marketing signs)

4.

5.

6.

7.

4. *"Front door landmark sculpture" is finished in gleaming white.*
5. *At night, lighting picks up sculptural elements of sign.*
6, 7. *Garage entrance bar and site regulatory signs are as low-key as possible.*
8. *Top detail of principal sculpture sign.*

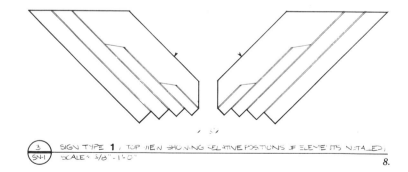

3
SN-1   SIGN TYPE **1** , TOP VIEW SHOWING RELATIVE POSITIONS OF ELEMENTS INSTALLED.
SCALE : 3/8" = 1'-0"

8.

Riverplace

Civic pride, a sense of history and a distinct understanding of the marketplace are all expressed in this mixed-use development that has come to life on the banks of the Mississippi. Occupying six acres along Main Street—site of the original city of Minneapolis—the development incorporates housing, offices, and 100,000 square feet of multi-level retail space centering on a historic warehouse and livery stable. Encompassed by skywalks, enhanced by greenhouse roofs, courtyards, fountains and cobbled streets, the development needed a graphic and signing system that would be festive, functional, and rooted in tradition. Indeed, the city's Historic Preservation Committee had exacting requirements for exterior graphics.

Designers D. I. Design and Development were determined to develop a solution that would be "dramatic and responsive to the riverfront location [in order] to reawaken the city of Minneapolis to its Mississippi River heritage and hitherto neglected birthplace. The design theme, therefore, makes full use of everything one might associate with the Mississippi River . . . from sternwheeler riverboats to cast-iron filigree, from period lighting to the innovative use of traditional finishes . . . all geared to emphasize and re-emphasize the rediscovery of the city's birthplace."

Since Riverplace is across the river from the main downtown area, the roof sign had to be large and brilliant enough to be clearly readable

from a distance by day and by night. The sign is 50′ long, is lit by 1500 lamps and uses 8′ and 6′-tall letters. The fabricated aluminum letters on the Greenhouse entrance are outlined in white 13mm neon. Neon and aluminum are used again in the 10′-diameter "One Main" sign, which is fabricated out of .090 aluminum and backlit by 13mm green neon. Letters are 2′ tall. The word "Riverplace" on this sign is not backlit, and the riverboat in the center is screen-printed on matte polycarbonate. Neon appears once again on the circular wall-mounted or free-standing public parking signs, which are constructed of .090 fabricated aluminum with acrylic faces. A blue neon "P" in the center remains lit at all times, but a "Lot Filled" sign in red pops on when appropriate.

One of the nicest features inside the retail space are the forty-nine 12″ globes indicating public amenities, phones, restrooms, and so on. Graphics here are either applied cut vinyl, or screened and then applied. The directories are either free-standing or mounted on pillars and are made of aluminum with borders of brass tubing. Hinged doors allow the screen-printed magnetic name strips to be readily changed or replaced as tenants come and go.

The designers were involved with the project for three years, a year of which time was devoted to detailed development of the signing program. Close collaboration with the fabricator, the Nordquist Sign Co., was a key factor in the successful realization of authentically-

1-3. Riverplace is a mixed use development incorporating a number of historic structures. Greenhouse roofs and covered walks make it inviting in the grimmest of Minnesota winters.

4.

5.

6.

7.

8.

9.

detailed, historically-inspired custom designs on such a large scale.

Chesterfield and Baskerville, the two typefaces used throughout the project, are also expressive of its historic associations.

Client: East Bank Riverfront Partners, Minneapolis
Design firm: D.I. Design & Development Consultants, Inc., Baltimore
Designer: Roy Higgs, partner-in-charge
Architects: Miller, Hanson Westerbeck Bell Architects, Inc.; Palaia-Svedburg Architects; Korsunsky Krank Erickson
Fabricator: Nordquist Sign Co.

4. *Fabricated aluminum letters on greenhouse entrance are outlined in white neon.*
5. *Lighted globes combine clear information with Old World charm.*
6. *Green neon illuminates the "One Main" sign.*
7. *Graceful old-time building details are restored and enhanced.*
8. *Free-flowing banners adorn the retail areas during Christmas 1985 season.*
9. *Mississippi steamboat recalls history of the site.*

10.

11.

12.

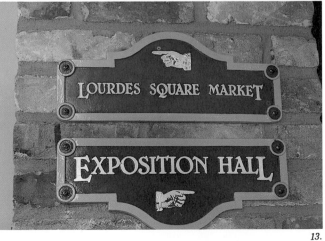

13.

10. Question-mark globe is a whimsical directory announcement.
11. Covered walks and bridges linking different parts of this large development are essential in a climate of temperature extremes.
12. Witty supergraphics enliven parking garage.
13. Directional signs reflect historic roots of development.

New Wilshire
Constuction Barricade

A brighter future for a somewhat run-down section of Los Angeles was confidently proclaimed via this construction fence, designed by Sidjakov Berman & Gomez to announce the forthcoming $40-million New Wilshire office building. Since the site is in one of the least desirable areas on the Wilshire Boulevard corridor, the name "New Wilshire" was chosen to convey a message of revitalization; and the construction fence had to try to sell the neighborhood's potential as well as the building itself. The slogan "the hardest working office building in Los Angeles" was intended to indicate the many amenities provided by the building for its prospective tenants.

An attractive *trompe-l'oeil* photo-mural of a street scene in which life-size, hand-painted people look for all the world like real pedestrians was capped by the 64½'-long draped logo, which seemed to be poised for unveiling. The effect was particularly dramatic in an area where there were not as yet many actual pedestrians, and especially so when real people did happen to walk past the painted figures. A businessman with a slight paunch, a mother tugging her unwilling child, an informal group in conference, a trendy couple out on a date were so very real that the street seemed to spring to life through their presence. The figures were derived from photos of actual city dwellers rendered in acrylic paint by Los Angeles artist and teacher Barry Fahr.

Construction of the barricade was quite complicated. The mural had to be in the form of movable panels (46 4'-by-8's) to allow construction crews to move equipment through and onto the site. Then, the fence had to be reinforced from behind to ensure that it could support the weight of the lettering in the event of high winds. The "New Wilshire" letters themselves (Bodoni Book, 5½' high and 1' deep) were cut out of wood and mounted on a wooden base. While the structure was lying flat, painter's canvas was draped over the lettering and glued flat to the letter faces, and then repainted to appear as close to its natural color as possible. The shadows of the draping and lettering were enhanced by airbrushing, and then the entire structure was coated with resin so that dust and pollution could be cleaned off from time to time. The mural was a black-and-white photoprint from 35mm film, mounted on a wood base, with color airbrushed on. This technique was used to ensure a consistently gray background. An anti-graffiti coating was applied, and apparently needed, since some vandalism did occur.

The results were gratifying, attracting both crowds and media coverage when first erected. The decision to create a street scene, rather than depict office equipment and activities, evidently paid off. *Casebook* jurors were particularly impressed by the visual effect of real people juxtaposed against their *trompe-l'oeil* counterparts. They also applauded a spirited revival of the genuine billboard.

1.

2.

1, 2. Construction barricade creates a trompe-l'oeil sidewalk scene on a hitherto rather barren section of Wilshire Boulevard.

Client: Mahoney-Sewell Associates, San Francisco
Design firm: Sidjakov Berman & Gomez, San Francisco
Designers: Jerry Berman, creative director; Barbara Vick, designer; Karen Emerson, production manager
Photographer: Charles Bush
Architect: William L. Pereira Associates
Fabricator: Siodmark Co., contractor; Serrurier & Associates, fabrication and installation

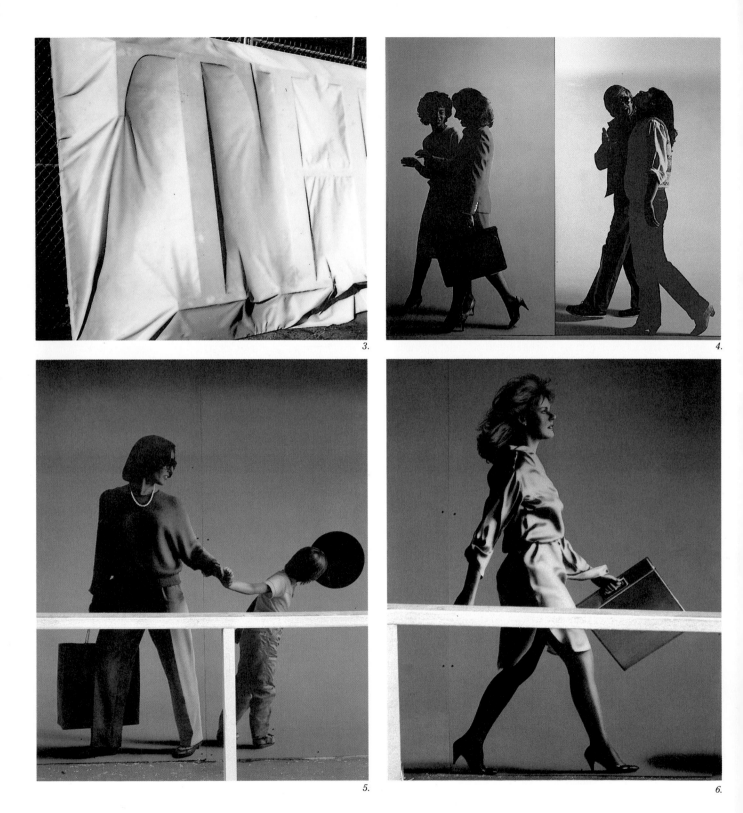

3.

4.

5.

6.

3. *Numerous draping studies were conducted to make canvas-draped letters of building logo appear ready for unveiling.*
4-6. *Photos of actual pedestrians form the basis of the* trompe-l'oeil *figures.*
7. *A real construction worker with a life-like strolling figure behind him.*

7.

Al Fresco
Restaurant

Denver's diners and strollers alike are fascinated by the violet metal ribbon that curves seductively in and out of the windowless frames of the facade of the booming Al Fresco restaurant. An undoubted factor in the huge success of the restaurant, the ribbon transforms the facade into street sculpture, enlivening the streetscape of a rejuvenated industrial section of the city.

The architecture of the restaurant lent itself to this daring solution, although the zoning regulations did not. The original building was completely gutted; but its brick facade was saved, and a new curved glass and stucco front set back behind it. This created an open space between the two walls—a perfect place to float a ribbon!

Brilliant in its originality and simplicity, the scheme was not easy to accomplish, since its implementation demanded considerable negotiation with city agencies, and then with potential fabricators. Designer Christina Weber describes the process: "The City of Denver has very strict zoning regulations that apply to signing in this lower downtown area. In order to obtain a revocable permit from the city that would allow us to encroach upon the public right-of-way (the sidewalk), we had to satisfy 12 special requirements and receive approval from the three other city department heads. Because of our tight time frame (six months), we had to accomplish this in record time with a minimum of red tape.

"The bidding process for fabrication and installation was complicated by the uniqueness of the design. Bids for construction ranged from $5000 to $30,000, with very divergent methods of fabrication and installation being proposed. The ribbon was finally installed on-site by two metal-workers who formed the curve of the ribbon as they connected it to the building. The old, unstable brick and decaying mortar made these connections complicated, and installation was accomplished after seven days of step-by-step problem-solving. The ribbon was painted after it was installed."

Sixteen-gauge steel sheet-metal was used for the 80 feet of 18'-wide ribbon. Polyester/polyurethane high-gloss paint was applied in a deep red-violet. Calligraphy for the Al Fresco logo was rendered in white hand-cut vinyl lettering.

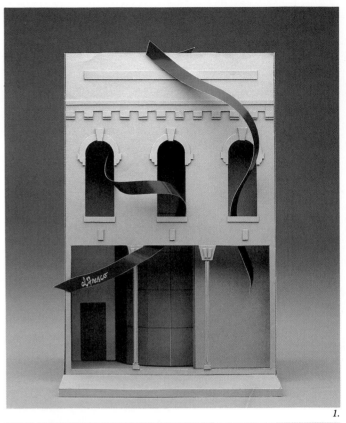

1.

1. Model of building facade with metal ribbon snaking through its vacant portals.
2. The curve of the ribbon had to be formed by the metal-workers who installed it.
3, 4. Brick front of gutted building was preserved to form a faux street facade. Restaurant's real curved-glass and brick-front wall is sheltered behind it.
5, 6. Ribbon sculpture is as dramatic from the restaurant as it is from the street.

Client: Giovanni and Janette Leone, Denver
Design firm: Weber Design, Denver
Designers: Christina Weber, Victoria Eubanks, Gail Slatter, Tamara Kudrycki
Architect: Morgan and Associates, Denver
Fabricator: Baird Metal, Inc.

2.

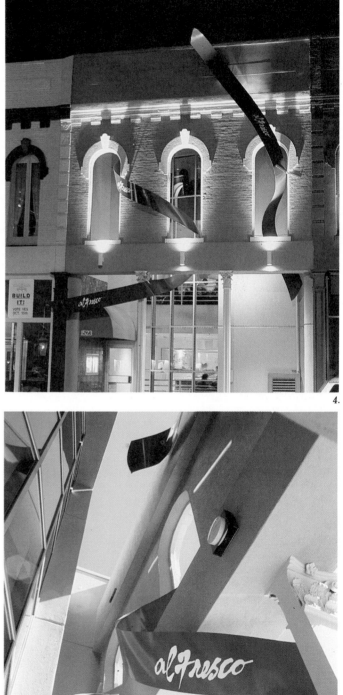

3.

4.

5.

6.

39/Environmental Graphics

1.

The romance of ocean liners remains, heightened by nostalgia now that their heyday as a form of transport is over. Some still do a thriving business as cruise ships, but it isn't quite the same. Nevertheless, it is encouraging to know that grand passenger ships are still being built, and the *Casebook* jury was interested to examine the elements of the signing system for the Niew Amsterdam and her sister ship the Noordam, and to learn what goes into such an undertaking.

Designers Bright & Associates are certainly the people to tell them, since their overall work for Holland America has involved them, since 1981, in the most extensive design program ever undertaken for the cruise industry . . . including 17,000 signs for a pair of cruise ships, consumer brochures, some of which had print runs of over a million copies, stateroom and barroom items, china, uniforms, posters, trade show exhibits, and on and on . . .

But the jury was concerned with two parts of the overall program which were handled as separate assignments: signing for the 1200-passenger ship the New Amsterdam (to be applied later to her sister ship the Noordam); and environmental and identifying signs for the Tampa, Florida, Holland America terminal, as well as identifying signs for buses. Some elements of this latter system—bus graphics, portable counters, and "roll-about" portable stanchions—were also manufactured for use in the company's facilities in other cities.

Work on the New Amsterdam signing started midway through the construction of the ship, and involved 7000 utility and safety signs, plus 30 various special-emphasis and theme signs. The program carried a design budget of approximately $450,000, and called for something "elegant, warm, readable, special, replaceable at sea."

After initial research, the designers divided the system into three elements: theme, utility and safety, and developed a vocabulary for each—gold leaf and various colors for special theme areas, brass and navy-blue type for utility signs, brass and red for safety. A redrawn corporate alphabet based on Caslon 540 was used for all messages to give consistency in a very varied environment. There was considerable range in sign sizes, the smallest being

2.

3.

only 3″ by 6″, the largest—the ship's name sign—being 40′ long.

A manual drawn up to guide and control fabrication of the numerous elements in the system was upgraded at the end of the process and then used as the basis for work on the Noordam.

The corporate typeface, a materials vocabulary of Panaflex, alucabond, canvas and brass, and a color palette of blue, white and corporate gray were used to extend the basic "look" and theme to Holland America's Tampa terminal and buses, and thence to the cruise line's on-shore facilities in other

American and Mexican cities. This time, there was a $100,000 design budget, and a three-month schedule for completion of the work.

The jury applauded the results of both parts of the program as "clear, fresh, optimistic, but with subtly handled recall of Art Deco, the 1920s and 1930s, when passenger ships were the last word in romance and elegance." The designers had clearly steeped themselves in Holland America's 100-year history, and in the whole machinery of cruise-going, with wholly laudable results.

Client: Holland Amerika Lijn, Rotterdam, The Netherlands; Holland America Line USA, Inc., Seattle (Noreen Young, director of creative services)
Design firm: Bright & Associates, Los Angeles
NIEW AMSTERDAM
Designers: Keith Bright, creative director; Raymond Wood, Mark Landkamer, John Guard, Peter Sargent, Michael Mills, designers; Kurt Klein, Suzi Poore, Vincent Debrito, Cathy Hennes, Jo Walker, Wynne Benit, production and coordination
Architect: Lawrence Zuidweg, Holland Amerika Lijn, Rotterdam
Consultants: Ken Parkhurst, alphabet and theme logo; Larry Klein
Fabricator: Thomas Swan Sign Co.
TERMINAL SIGNING
Designers: Larry Klein, Dean Alexander, John Guard
Architect: Reynolds, Smith & Hills
Consultant: Geoff Siodmark
Fabricator: Heath & Co.

4.

1. Nieuw Amsterdam *at anchor.*
2, 3. *Color-coded luggage tags and life boat-station signs are but two elements in the most extensive graphics program ever undertaken for the cruise industry.*
4. *Original Holland America symbol was retained. It depicts Henry Hudson's* Half Moon *alongside an ocean liner.*

5.

6.

7.

8.

9.

10.

11.

12.

13.

14.

5, 6. *Historical themes are illustrated in restaurant and casino signs.*

7. *Caslon 540, modified and customized as corporate type, is executed in gold leaf on glass to announce the ship's pool and gymnasium complex.*

8-10. *Ship's signs, numbering 17,000 for two liners, range in size from 3" by 6" to 40', and all use the corporate typeface.*

11, 12, 14. *The same typeface is used for site identification, dockside information kiosk and gift shop designed for all American and Mexican Holland America terminals.*

13. *Annual world cruise poster for 1984. (Illustration by Raymond Wood.)*

Plane Mate

Eight newly-purchased vehicles in the Port Authority of New York and New Jersey's Plane Mate fleet of people movers not only carry people between their planes and the International Arrivals Building at Kennedy Airport, but also proclaim the city's welcome in boldly rendered graphic terms. Moving on from the "New York Loves You" message on the initial vehicle (see *Environmental Graphics Casebook 6*, pages 55-57), designer Diane Whitebay has used symbols of the city on bright red, green, yellow, orange and blue backgrounds to convey the same feeling. The Big Apple, the Statue of Liberty, the Brooklyn Bridge and the New York skyline appear most dramatic on the sides of the lumbering 49'-long, 15'-high, 15'-wide vehicles, and in case there was any doubt, let even those passengers arriving in a fog know exactly where they are.

Considerable study was needed in the positioning of the graphics, since they have to be seen from many angles and substantial distances and be clearly legible from the control tower. The vehicles' cabs themselves are raised and lowered to get people on and off the plane. All of this mandated a simple solution, but everyone wanted to inject some variety and excitement by going beyond the original typographic message . . . with great success, thought the *Casebook* jury. In addition to the pictorial symbols, each vehicle carries the Port Authority's logo and a large identifying letter—24" high on the vehicle's side, 6' on its roof.

Once the concept was approved, Diane Whitebay prepared a drawing detailing symbol and type sizes, spacing and positioning, and then a precise mechanical which was enlarged to full size and used as artwork.

The vehicles were built in Pennsylvania and shipped in sections to New York, where the paint and white vinyl graphics were applied. The wide bodies made shipping awkward and there was much denting, scratching and breaking of windows that had to be taken care of before the finish was applied. Helvetica Extra Bold was used for the identifying letters. All graphics are white, except for the red apple on the green vehicle, and the green apple on the red one.

1. Poster combining New York symbols and color palette used to enliven Plane Mate vehicles.
2, 4. Statue of Liberty face on blue and red vehicles.
3, 5. Brooklyn Bridge in white on green.
6-9. Symbols forming basis of Plane Mate decoration.

Client: Port Authority of New York and New Jersey, Aviation Dept., New York City (Robert J. Aaronson, director)
Design firm: Port Authority of New York and New Jersey, Engineering Dept., New York City (Rino M. Monti, director of engineering/chief engineer)
Designer: Diane Whitebay, graphic designer
Architect: Sheldon D. Wander, chief architect, Port Authority of New York and New Jersey; Maria Aasland, interior designer
Consultants: Port Authority of New York and New Jersey, Central Automotive Div., General Services Dept.
Fabricators: Ariston, Inc. (graphics); Airside Systems, Inc. (vehicles)

1.

6.

2.

3.

4.

5.

7.

8.

9.

10.

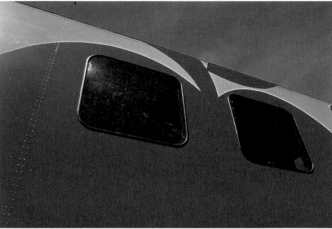

11.

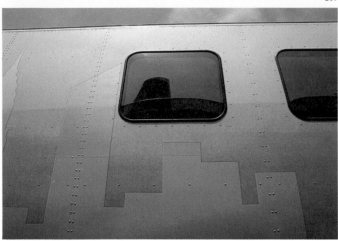

12.

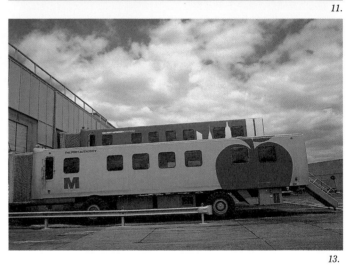

13.

10, 12. *New York City skyline rendered on*
   sides of vehicle.
11, 13. *The "Big Apple" in red on green.*

Horton Plaza

If the Pacific Rim verve and imagery, and the pervasive sense of fiesta, that colored the Los Angeles Olympics (see page 64) seem to be present at Horton Plaza, this is no accident. The same design team—the Jerde Partnership, with graphic consultation from Sussman/Prejza—were responsible for this 11½-acre "urban experience" in the heart of downtown San Diego. Covering 6½ city blocks, and incorporating several restored historic buildings, this ambitious mixed-use complex—with 900,000 sq. ft. of multi-level retail space—has transformed a somewhat down-at-heel section and become the shopping pulse of the city.

In a country where shopping might plausibly be described as the national sport, Jon Jerde promised the users of Horton Plaza an experience in some ways more European than American—with meandering streets, dense urban texture, banners, warm pastel colors, surprises at every corner, numerous places to dine or sit and enjoy a Vermouth Cassis or an ice cream soda. To achieve just the ambience he had in mind, Jerde and his team developed unusually stringent, yet highly innovative, tenant design criteria, which would in fact force the 160 tenants to obey both the spirit and the letter of the design laws. The four main design objectives set out in a summary statement demand that
• store designs must reflect an urban context;
• standard store images must be creatively adapted;
• a total store design must be developed;
• the customer experience must be enhanced.

To further these ends, Horton Plaza was divided into ten districts, each with its own set of design criteria to establish a sense of place.

The Palazzo, a historic triangular building—restored with a dramatic facade retreatment in mosaic tile—required its tenant stores to strive for "high quality with a rich but conservative look." The South Terrace, on the other hand, imposed a "bright, casual Southern Californian attitude and image," while the Colonnade encouraged "creative expression of theme elements in a three-dimensional form."

Hallmark, for example, a tenant of the Colonnade district, had to abandon its traditional imagery to come up with a "theme-oriented storefront, animating some aspect of either the function of the space or the type of product to be sold." The result: a facade incorporating an oversize pen, paper clip, rubber stamp, and so on, that still somehow contrived to maintain the prescribed vocabulary of "painted or stained wood facade, polished metals, such as brass or bronze, and a storefront color scheme emphasizing the natural tones of the materials used."

In Restaurant Row, much more apparent freedom is allowed to give patrons a wide choice of dining ambience. Here, tenants are asked to "establish their own architectural character and identity within the urban and architectural context of Horton Plaza." But to ensure that each is perceived as a different building, "tenants must extend their architecture up to and even beyond the existing roof parapet."

The urban and architectural context of Horton Plaza includes, in addition to an amazing variety of specialty stores and restaurants, a hotel, an office tower, a theater, a collection of street sculpture (including the famous Jessop Clock with its 20 dials — moved to Horton Plaza with Jessops Jewelry Store), and surely somewhere a Punch and Judy show.

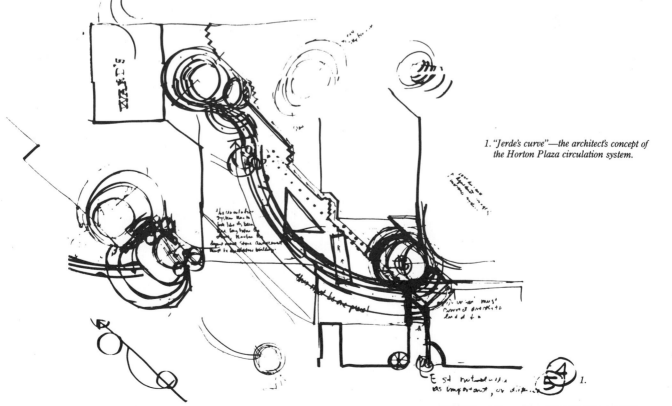

1. "Jerde's curve"—the architect's concept of the Horton Plaza circulation system.

2. *Model shows the curve in urban context.*
3. *Model shows the plaza come-to-life.*
4. *Antique clock moved to Horton Plaza with Jessop's Jewelry Store.*
5. *View showing multi-level activity.*
6. *Texture, color and ornament—three Post-Modern themes.*
7. *Dramatic use of ceramic tile on restored building facades.*
8, 9. *(Page 50) Mosaics, banners, lion's head and industrial details—the influence of several cultures.*
10, 11. *(Page 50) A bird's-eye view and a convocation.*

Client: Ernest W. Hahn, Inc., San Diego, CA
Design firm: The Jerde Partnership, Los Angeles
Architect: The Jerde Partnership, Inc.
Consultant: Sussman/Prejza (color/signing)
Fabricator: Nu-Hahn Construction

2.

3.

4.

5.

6.

7.

8.

9.

10.

11.

Four pavilions, connected by an arched skylit mall, have given Californians yet another new experience in the growing repertoire of shoppers' attractions being unveiled for the American public. Despite all the delights of the newest shopping malls, Jon Jerde of the Jerde Partnership, architects for the West Side Pavilion and other significant people-oriented environments, feels that many people are still hesitant to do their everyday shopping in a mall. The size intimidates them (West Side, for example, has 300,000 sq. ft. of shops, restaurants and boulevard boutiques). They find the parking arrangements inconvenient, and are often confused about how to get to and from their cars. They are afraid that there won't be enough small specialty shops to give them the kinds of choices they need. They wonder if there will be anything else to do besides shop. Having gone to all the trouble of parking their cars in the garage, they want to be able to have lunch or coffee and keep their children occupied while they find out what the mall has to offer.

Drawing upon European and neo-classical architectural elements, and the soft, warm colors of the southwest, Jerde has done much to counteract these fears, and provide an "inviting open-air continental shopping district, oriented to the window shopping, strolling pedestrian." Since many of the shops open onto the already active Los Angeles westside streetscape, as well as onto the interior mall, West Side Pavilion does not feel like a contrived environment completely cut off from the city-at-large. Alive with banners, canopies, outdoor restaurants, and street furniture, it has the aura of a 19th-century European shopping arcade, elegant and sheltered, but very much part of city life.

Parking is well handled in four separate garages directly tied in to the retail space.

The *Casebook* jurors were particularly struck by the successful logo—based on the arch of the greenhouse roof—that is applied with equal élan at the grand scale of the major mall entrances, and to printed material. The large gilt "W," mounted on tiles, is surrounded by the word "West Side" within the arc of the roof. Gold cross-hatching and a tile border fill the center of the arc, and the word "Pavilion" is spelled out across the bottom on a green/blue background.

West Side Pavilion, in the view of the jury, demonstrates some of the most attractive characteristics of the Jerde approach—use of neo-classical elements, warm pastel colors, ceramic tile, and an ability to combine European, Pacific Rim and Art Deco themes with vim and vigor, but without too much confusion or garishness. This is no doubt partly because, as at Horton Plaza (see page 47), he insists on carefully drawn up tenant guidelines, and manages to see that these are strictly enforced.

1.

2.

1. Convenient juxtaposition of parking, street access and sheltered retail pavilions helps to overcome shopper's resistance to the "mall" concept.
2. Skylit mall recalls 19th-century European shopping arcades.

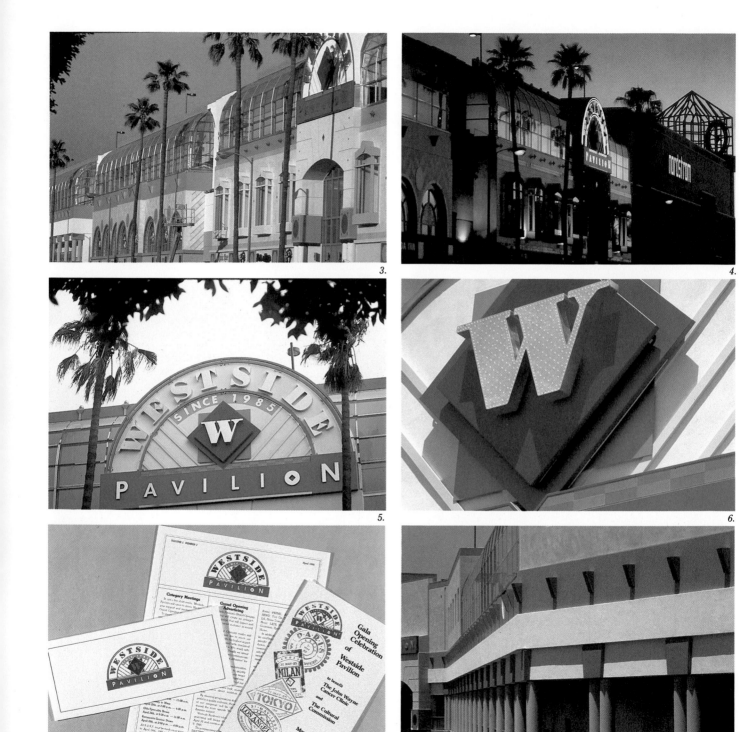

3.

4.

5.

6.

7.

8.

9.

10.

3,4. Many shops open onto street as well as
   to mall.
5-7. Logo works as well for major building
   identification as for printed matter.
8. A new interpretation of the colonnade.
9. Easy access to street.
10. The skylit mall by night.

Client: Westfield, Inc., Santa Monica,
CA
Design firm: The Jerde Partnership,
Inc., Los Angeles
Architect: The Jerde Partnership
Graphic consultant: Sussman/
Prejza, Inc.
Fabricator: Westfield, Inc.
(contractors)

Rockefeller Center

Rockefeller Center's ambitious new signing program has culminated in the installation in the 11 building lobbies of an electronic tenant directory system, consisting of 12 wall-mounted and five free-standing cabinets, that gives instant push-button public access to some 25,000 tenants. A network of 48 computer display screens and one control terminal have replaced the massive existing wall directories, and by so doing have created the space and the opportunity for an accompanying art program. The design and fabrication firm of Public Access Systems came up with the idea of reproducing some of the Center's most famous public art on large glass panels incorporated with the directories. Accordingly, having convinced the client of the wisdom of the idea, they devised a technique for achieving a three-dimensional rendition by cutting the reproductions into ½"-thick glass and then painting or gilding them over. It was this that especially won the *Casebook* jury's admiration.

For each of the 17 artworks involved, a precise stencil was drawn from a photograph and then transferred to masking material adhered to the glass. The masking material was cut along the stencil lines, peeled away and then the glass sandblasted. A variety of hose nozzles and pressures were used in the process, and credit for the accuracy of the results must be given to the discerning eyes of the designers. The art chosen for display is that which appears most prominently on the facade or over entrances of

the buildings concerned. Among the famous works reproduced are "Light" and "Sound," two polychromatic limestone panels from the RCA Building entrance, the 10-ton stainless steel panel "News" by Isamu Noguchi above the 50 Rockefeller Plaza entrance to the Associated Press Building, and "St. Francis of Assissi Feeding Birds," a limestone panel by Lee Lawrie, which appears above one of the entrances to the International Building.

Materials used in the directory system—brass, black glass, plexiglass, aluminum—and green lettering generally continue the vocabulary successfully established by Donovan and Green in an earlier phase of the resigning program (see *Environmental Graphics Casebook 6*, pages 46, 47). The artwork is finished in gold leaf, silver leaf, paint and bronze powder.

The wall-mounted cases range in size from 3′ by 7′ to 4′ by 20′, and all are 1′1″ deep where they accommodate the directory monitors. But they are reduced to only a 6″ depth where the artwork alone is housed in order to lessen their bulky appearance as far as possible. The free-standing cases measure 2′8″ square by 6′4″ tall. Here, the monitors were positioned off-center to allow a 4″ reduction in both the width and depth of the casework.

In order to avoid chaos in the lobbies while the new system was being installed, barricades were erected around each installation point, and the old directories mounted on them for the duration of the

electronic and construction work. Before the system was implemented, a three-screen prototype including artwork was installed and surveyed by Rockefeller Center personnel and a series of consultants for a period of some nine months to test effectiveness, reliability and image.

The system, which is cross-referenced, has the capacity to cover more than double the existing number of tenants, and to provide information on upcoming Rockefeller Center events (for example, the traditional lighting of the Christmas Tree). Integrated information panels provide directions for use in five languages.

Client: The Rockefeller Group, New York City
Design firm: Public Access Systems, New York City
Designers: Eric Silverstein, Deborah Gutow
Architect: Jim Smith/ The Rockefeller Group
Fabricator: Public Access Systems

1. *New York's famed Rockefeller Center.*
2. *Kiosk directory at 1230 Sixth Avenue incorporates panels depicting a smokestack and eagle representing modern ages of the industrialized republic.*
3. *"News" depicts five figures using the tools of the press—from Associated Press Building.*
4. *Wall-mounted directory in RCA Building incorporates art panel depicting "Light" as a female figure.*
5. *Detail of "Four Human Races" from International Building.*

1.

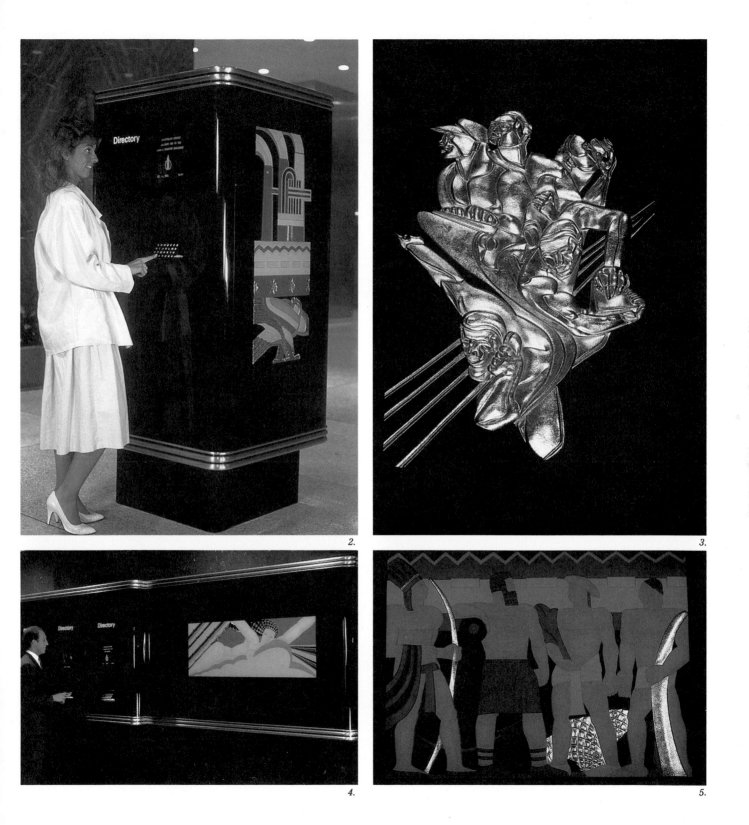

2.

3.

4.

5.

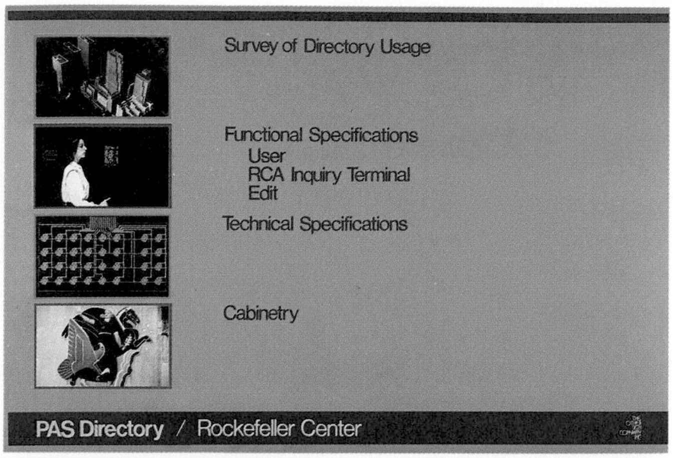
Survey of Directory Usage
Functional Specifications
User
RCA Inquiry Terminal
Edit
Technical Specifications
Cabinetry
PAS Directory / Rockefeller Center

6.

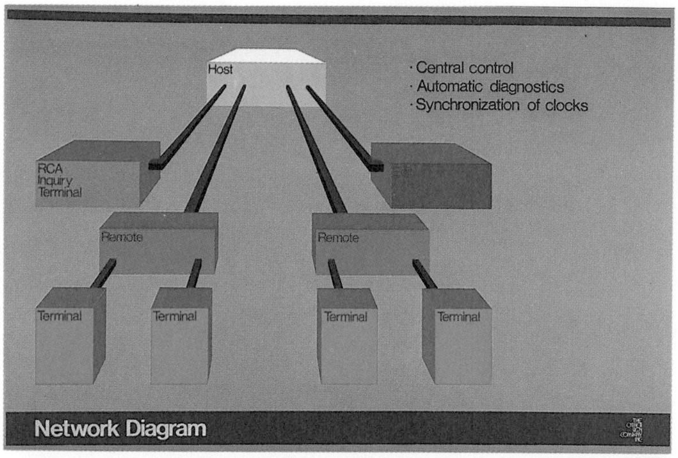
Host
· Central control
· Automatic diagnostics
· Synchronization of clocks
RCA
Inquiry
Terminal
Remote
Remote
Terminal
Terminal
Terminal
Terminal
Network Diagram

7.

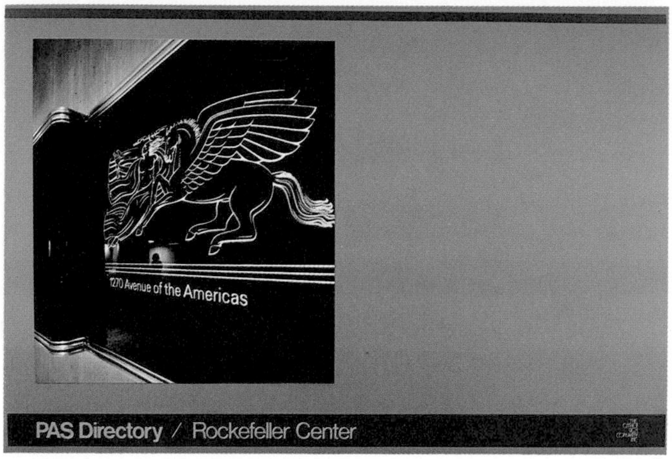
1270 Avenue of the Americas
PAS Directory / Rockefeller Center

8.

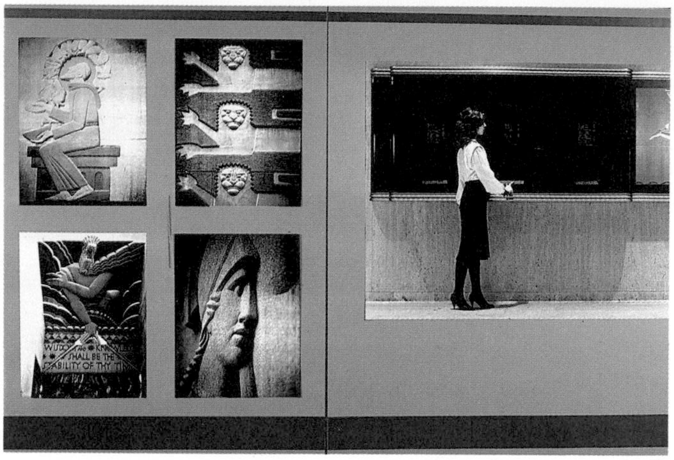

9.

6-9. Stages in evolution of the electronic directory system.

City of Charlotte, North Carolina

The City of Charlotte is the largest metropolis in the Carolinas, and its efforts to use graphic design to enhance its image were applauded by the *Casebook* jurors, who understood only too well the difficulties of budget and bureaucracy that can so easily reduce such programs to mediocrity. In this case, budget limitations seem to have had a salutary effect in producing a signing system that is clear, attractive, flexible and easy to apply and maintain. It is also appropriate to the architecture and history of the place.

Since the city was named for England's Queen Charlotte, the crown was a logical logo design, and is now used on city-owned property from stationery and uniforms to signs and vehicles. In addition to creating this logo, designers Yasuhiko Taguchi and Mary Head of Design/Joe Sonderman, Inc., were asked to establish basic design standards and guidelines for application and maintenance. The first application of the signing system was to the Government Plaza and to the city's motor vehicles. The installation at the city government complex was viewed as a prototpye for expanded use of the system in government facilities throughout the city.

By establishing a system of painted, square tubular posts, and painted .125-aluminum-sheet sign surfaces, the designers gave the city the flexibility to employ double-post signs with single or double faces, and single-post signs with a range of from one to four panels. The edge of each graphic panel is bent 45

1. *Crown logo for the city, namesake of England's Queen Charlotte, wife of George III.*
2. *Single-post signs can have from one to four panels.*

1.

2.

degrees and mounted on the post with self-tapped screws. All graphics are either screened or reflective vinyl. Two basic colors—burgundy for buildings, green for vehicular and pedestrian-oriented signs—work well in a city where natural brick and lush greenery characterize the public/government precincts.

The logo and Univers type are in white throughout. Univers was chosen as a contrast to the stylized type on the logo itself.

Some of the building signs are wall-mounted, others are double-post signs—6′6″ high, 4′ wide, and 2½″ deep. The City Hall sign is 8′ high, 5′9″ wide and 1′6″ deep.

3.

3. Logo applied to shirt patch for sanitation worker.
4. Sketch showing location of major government center sign.
5, 6. The logo applied to city-owned vehicles.
7, 8. White on burgundy is the color scheme for building-related signs, to complement a predominantly brick and stone building vocabulary.
9. Square tubular post and aluminum panel sign system with single or double posts has versatile application.

Client: City of Charlotte, NC
Design firm: Design/Joe Sonderman, Inc., Charlotte, NC
Designers: Yasuhiko Taguchi, Mary Head
Fabricator: Graphic Systems/International, Inc.

4.

5.

6.

7.

8.

9.

An unusually responsive architect-client-designer relationship was the key factor in the success of this signing and directory system for the new 365-room Sheraton Hotel, an encouraging new presence in a still run-down but fast redeveloping area of downtown Tacoma, Washington. The client was quite clear about what was wanted—a graphic response to the elegance of the architecture and interior design which would be easy to read but low-key, would use a neutral color palette, and could be accomplished within a tight budget. Six months were allowed for completion of the project within a total projected cost of $70,000.

The high central lobby/atrium of the hotel was furnished in soft, warm colors with furniture that displayed some oriental and Art Deco influences. The graphic design responded with a scheme that picks up the black lacquer of the furniture, and copper railing building details, but does not intrude upon the guests' perception of the architecture.

The TRA graphic design team decided to simplify their concept by reducing the amount of hardware involved. They therefore dispensed with sign panels for the most part, and opted for individual cut-out letters mounted directly on strategic architectural surfaces. Since the building surfaces offered only limited room for signs, this forced an economy and restraint, which the designers feel was altogether beneficial in the long run.

Black gloss acrylic sheet—simulating the lacquer finish on the furniture—was used for the

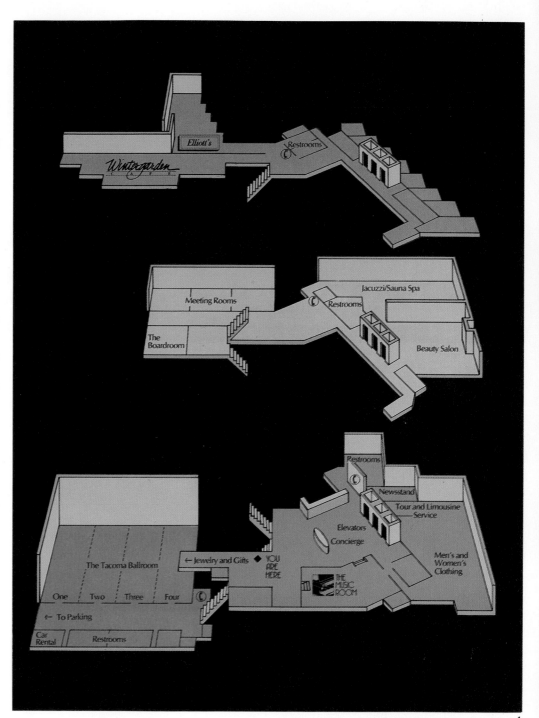

1.

1. *Exploded view of public spaces in the hotel, which forms part of lobby directory (see Fig. 10, page 63).*
2. *Registration sign shows use of architectural surface for direct mounting of cutout letters.*
3. *Diamond-shaped acrylic guest room signs have copper foil numbers.*
4. *Where sign plaques are needed, they are made of clear acrylic sheet to minimize visual clutter.*
5. *Rose Room sign is wall-mounted and enhanced by subtle lighting.*

2.

3.

4.

5.

61/Environmental Graphics

cut-out letters. Copper was used on selected letters marking the ballroom, where it reflects the dominant interior detailing of the area. The copper railing motif was incorporated in the directory, which also has a changeable fabric menu board, and backlighting for the 3D map and restaurant advertisements. Diamond-shaped acrylic signs with copper foil numbers impart distinction to the guest room doors. Where wall plaque room signs are used, they are made of clear acrylic sheet with polished edges and screened images on the reverse to intrude as little as possible on the interior environment. Capone Light, the Sheraton corporate typeface, and Optima Light for small text constitute the type vocabulary. The main function labels are 8″ caps with letterspace and diamond spacers. General directional signs to shops and the like are 4″ upper- and lower-case.

Some problems arose in achieving the right quality of fabrication, which required constant supervision on the part of the designers and the help of another contractor. The client, deeply involved, was nonetheless understanding, and "threw a terrific opening party for the design team."

Client: Cornerstone Development Co., Seattle
Design firm: TRA Graphic Design, Seattle
Designers: Kelly Brandon, project director; Mark Koch, project manager; Carole Jones, Mike Marshall
Architect: TRA Architecture Engineering Planning Interiors, Seattle
Fabricator: Tacoma Rubber Stamp Co.

6. *Thumbnail sketches of major services and activities.*
7, 8. *Services/activity pictograms derived from thumbnails.*
9. *Sheraton logo on building exterior.*
10. *Lobby directory has three components—exploded view of public spaces (see Fig. 1); menu board of activities; and advertising panel for restaurants and other hotel amenities.*
11-14. *Except in rare cases, signing is applied directly to architectural surfaces.*

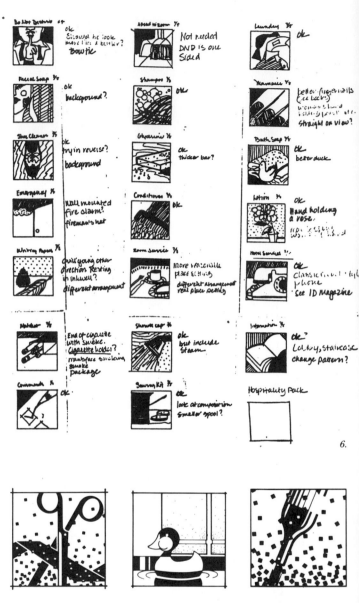

6.

7.

8.

9.

10.

EXECUTIVE
OFFICES

11.

← TO MEETING ROOMS
CAFE AND BAR

← TO THE TACOMA BALLROOM

12.

Wintergarden
C A F E

13.

R E G I S T R A T I O N

14.

1984 Los Angeles Olympics

One of the advantages of the *Print Casebooks'* biennial schedule is that sometimes quite major projects are reviewed after they have been widely publicized and are already well-known to the members of the jury. This provides opportunities for an objective "second look," a balanced post-design judgment, a chance to assess design impact from the perspective of time and familiarity.

Now that the "tumult and the shouting" surrounding the 1984 Los Angeles Olympics have died, how does its image and much-heralded environmental design program hold up? This was the question the *Casebook* jurors asked themselves, as the overall Olympic "look," and two families of application of the established theme to particular aspects of the environment, were presented to them for review.

The verdict in favor was enthusiastic, and all but unanimous. Essentially temporary in nature, this extraordinary example of the art and applications of environmental graphics, sometimes called "graphic architecture," had, in the jury's view, stood the test of time, and would remain in the imagination as long as the events themselves were remembered.

1.

2.

Overall Program

Two firms—the Jerde Partnership and the Sussman/ Prejza Company—working in close and creative collaboration, were responsible for the overall "look" and much of the implementation that, in the words of one design editor, "covered the city of Los Angeles with a temporary blanket of color and materials based around a kit of colors and a kit of parts."

The color palette, staying firmly away from patriotic red, white and blue and leaning on the influence of the Pacific Rim—Mexico and the Orient— unfolded in a panoply of vibrant magenta, vermilion, aqua and chrome yellow, with secondary and tertiary shades of yellow, green, lavender, light blue, violet, blue and pink. The effect was hot, bright, entirely festive and immediately recognizable. Spreading out from the center

of activities to the streets and freeways of Southern California, the colors lit up the environment, drawing people to the games either as participants or observers.

The Jerde Partnership and Sussman/Prejza scheme had to concern itself with 28 different sports venues, 42 Arts Festival locations, and three Olympic Villages, as well as the aforementioned streets and freeways. It had to provide strong identity, but encourage almost infinite variety, and be capable of interpretation and application by numerous firms, organizations and individuals— sometimes working with little direct supervision from the original designers.

Limited time and budget stringencies, plus the Los Angeles climate, favored the notion of a vocabulary of temporary architectural

elements that could create a whole world of its own, vivid, alive, durable for the duration, but essentially ephemeral in nature.

Sonotube columns (the forms without the concrete), rental tents with "witch's hat" or pyramidal tops, building blocks, scaffolding, chain-link fencing (painted or fabric-covered) and a "confetti" of plywood cutouts, fiberglass spheres, banners, and a sophisticated signing system juxtaposed the color palette against the background of everyday Los Angeles life, so that everything to do with the Olympics seemed to be in another dimension.

The colors also provided identifying coding. Sports pictograms, for example, were always in white on a magenta background; freeway signs were magenta with aqua; and the different competition sites had

their own color schemes within the palette. Gymnastics were vermilion, chrome yellow and green; swimming used fields of aqua and white. Stripes were layered thin against thick, light against dark, so that repetition need not be relentless, nor recognition boring.

The architectural components were built into structures—sometimes elaborate and fanciful, sometimes evocative. The jury thought the Sonotubes were especially effective, creating colonnades and arbors, avenues and portals—a consistent but immensely varied framework for the theater of people and events.

The resources of Los Angeles with all the ingenuity of Hollywood at its disposal were perfectly fitted for the construction of so dramatic and ephemeral a city.

1,2. Drawings on 3" by 5" cards develop a "pattern language" of architectural and graphic elements.
3. Print graphics combine color palette and Olympic symbolism.
4. Facade of Exposition Park.

5.

6.

7.

8.

9.

10.

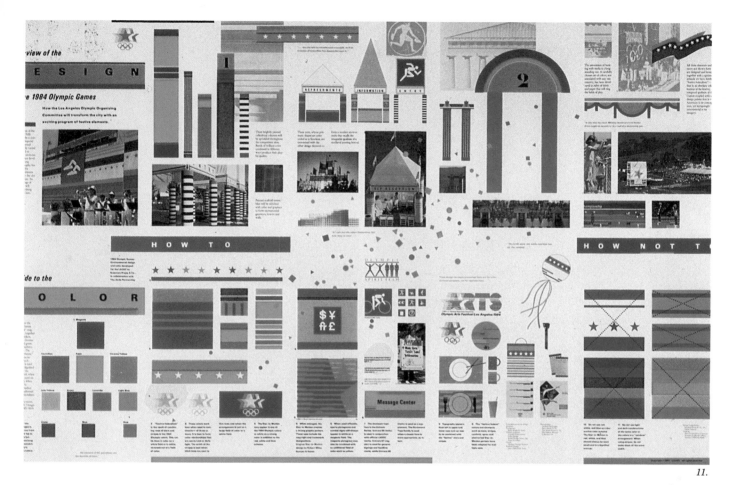

11.

5. *Olympic symbol on chain-link fence.*
6. *Olympic sign atop Los Angeles street signing system is immediately recognizable by its colors.*
7. *A temple of Sonotubes overlooks water sports venue.*
8. *Quarter-round tent tops on zebra columns mark the entry to sports venues.*
9. *Graphic announcement of public amenities.*
10. *Fabric-wrapped fence in swimming area.*
11. *Design and color guide explains "kit of parts" to a large design team.*
12. *Early, fanciful study for street banner.*

Client: Los Angeles Olympic Organizing Committee (LAOOC)
Design firms: The Jerde Partnership, Inc., Los Angeles (Jon Jerde, David Meckel); Sussman/Prejza & Co., Santa Monica, CA (Deborah Sussman, Paul Prejza)
Consultant: Larry Klein, LAOOC Graphic Design Dept.

12.

13.

15.

14.

16.

Street Decoration Program

The banners that proved to be the most conspicuous part of the Olympic urban decoration program were the work of the design firm of Hinsche & Associates, collaborating, of course, with the Jerde-Sussman/Prejza team, and Larry Klein of LAOOC.

Working within the established vocabulary, the designers created banners which could literally be clipped onto existing street furniture for a period of four to six weeks and then easily removed. The initial $1,000,000 budget for this part of the Olympics program was considerably expanded after initial installations were made, to allow neighboring municipalities to participate.

In the short (four-month) schedule allowed for the work, Hinsche & Associates mapped and surveyed the streets and routes to the major games and arts venues, examined fabrication methods and materials and studied city ordinances. All this was very necessary, as fabrics and colors had to be decided on and ordered before design development was complete in order to meet the deadlines. Some fabric and color combinations, it turned out, would only have a two-week street life. City codes limited the overall banner sizes allowed, resulting in a 3' by 8' size for most of them, and occasional comments from critics that the banners might have been larger to good effect.

More than 20,000 nylon banners with aluminum fixtures were produced, covering more than 125 miles of Los Angeles streets and equal mileage in other cities. The numbers and frequency of the banners were intensified in the immediate vicinity of major venues of the Games.

Client: Los Angeles Olympic Organizing Committee (Larry Klein, design director; Pat Murray, coordinator)
Design firm: Hinsche & Associates, Santa Monica, CA
Designers: James Guerard, John Tom, Gary Hinsche
Olympic Design Team: The Jerde Partnership, Los Angeles; Sussman/ Prejza, Santa Monica
Fabricator: Pageantry World

13. Awning over bus station.
14. Wizard's hat information tent.
15. Monumental gateway and information kiosk at one of the Olympic Villages.
16. Blackboard showing scale, color and hierarchy of Olympic signs.
17. Page from brochure developed to explain street banners to other municipalities who wanted to participate.

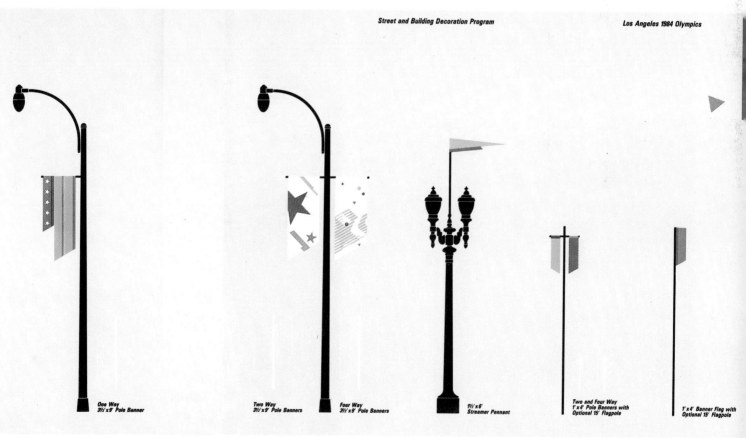

Street and Building Decoration Program   Los Angeles 1984 Olympics

One Way
3½' x 9' Pole Banner

Two Way
3½' x 9' Pole Banners

Four Way
3½' x 9' Pole Banners

1½' x 6'
Streamer Pennant

Two and Four Way
1' x 4' Pole Banners with
Optional 15' Flagpole

1' x 4' Banner Flag with
Optional 15' Flagpole

17.

18.

19.

20.

21.

22.

23.

18-24. Banners and their application throughout L.A. environs. All were designed for easy attachment to existing light standards or architectural elements.

24.

Arts Festival

In association with the Olympic Design Team, Hinsche + Associates were also responsible for applying the Olympic "look" to 28 of the Arts Festival locations, with once again little more than a four-month schedule, a design budget of $45,000 and a construction budget of $450,000.

All the sites were visited, documented and photographed, and the "kit of parts" described above applied where it would create maximum impact without detracting from or physically damaging the original architecture; however, some drilling into buildings was necessary to firmly anchor the temporary structures. A lot of the decisions had to be somewhat *ad hoc*, since there was no time for testing at the sites. Materials used were plywood for the cutouts, nylon and aluminum "confetti," nylon and vinyl banners and vinyl fencing. Colors were within the established palette.

The star—taken, of course, from the American flag to figure in the basic Olympic vocabulary—was applied with dramatic effect in some of the Arts Festival locations.

Despite its international intent and flavor, "America" and "LA" intentionally read clearly through the whole program, which did in fact contribute to the widespread expression of national pride aroused by the Summer Games of 1984.

Client: Los Angeles Olympic Organizing Committee (Larry Klein, design director; Pat Murray, Coordinator)
Design firm: Hinsche + Associates, Santa Monica, CA
Designers: Gary Hinsche, James Guerard, John Tom, Scott Cuyler (Sussman/Prejza)
Olympic Design Team: The Jerde Partnership, Los Angeles; Sussman/Prejza & Co., Santa Monica, CA

25, 26. Working drawing and actual application of "Olympic look" to Arts Festival venue.
27-30. Free-standing, as a fabric-covered fence, or attached to a building facade, the star symbol of America and the Olympiad was applied with dramatic effect in some Arts Festival locations.
31. Typical presentation made to Arts Festival venue-owners to show where and how Olympic elements would be applied. Detailed installation instructions were then developed.

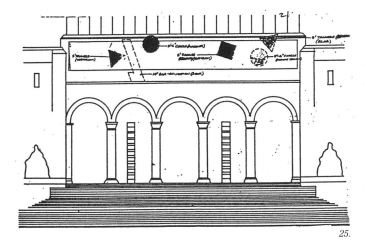

25.

26.

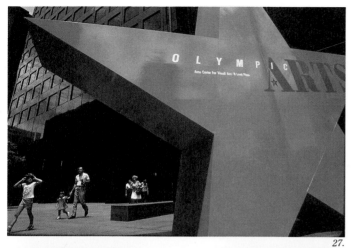

27.

28.

29.

30.

Allied Chemical Plant

In an era when deserted industrial buildings are being converted into all manner of things, from apartments to artists' studios to specialty shopping marts, laudable though this activity is, it is refreshing to contemplate an *active* plant—anxious to enchance its image, but resolved not to hide its industrial character in the process. The vast Allied Chemical chrome-producing plant, a prominent presence in Baltimore's newly revitalized Inner Harbor, needed a better image that would stress its role as a conscientious neighbor, and reinforce its physical identity. Since the building was due for its biennial chemical cleaning and repainting, this offered an opportunity to make the painting process the means for image enchancement. The design firm of Land Design/ Research, brought in initially as design consultant, was retained as designer to carry out the facade improvement program.

The somber presence of this enormous plant, which is never without some sounds of activity, was characterized by the designers as a "snoring mammoth," and they wanted its new image to capitalize on its strength, rather than move away from or try to hide it. The impressive massing of the dark building against the changing colors of sky and water was the inspiration for their solution, in which the building's silhouette is repeated as three broad bands of gray paint, deepening in shade as they descend. The building had been gray for several years before the enhancement program, and gray seemed to complement the characteristic pale gray Maryland sky, and the steel-gray waters of the Baltimore harbor. Says designer Cynthia L. Hanegraaf, "The painting of the buildings enhanced the view without transforming the plant into an attraction. The inherent grace and dignity of the industrial complex was emphasized rather than hidden."

Over 82,000 square feet of surface area is exposed to the Inner Harbor. The surface is predominantly corrugated asbestos panels, but there are exposed steel beams, pieces of heavy machinery and storage tanks covered with insulating material that had to be incorporated into the scheme. Although the treatment of corners and different planes was carefully worked out in the drawings, the designers admit that "in several instances, sections of the facade had to be repainted to visually correct solutions that had worked on paper but not in the field." In most cases the roofs were not painted, except on the south face where the roof is so low, large and visible that to omit it would disrupt the unity of the scheme. Here, the width of the bands was increased on the inclined plane until they now appear to match those on the adjoining vertical surfaces.

A special paint had to be made that would adhere to this variety of materials and surfaces, and maintenance will require washing with high-pressure water jets every few months.

In addition to studies of the building, which included a photo-survey carried out from a garbage scow in the harbor, the

1.

1-3. The designers prepared a series of display boards explaining concept and its implementation.
4. View of the Allied Building in its Inner Harbor context.
5. Building silhouette at sunrise — the charms of industrial architecture — inspired a painting design that repeated the building contours in deepening bands of color.

What's Going On Over There?

Paint is what is going on. And it is going on to the Baltimore Works of the Allied Chemical Corporation. Painting a chemical plant isn't unusual. Part of regular maintenance is to give large industrial operations a new coat every year or so. The difference between Allied's new coat and the one it had before is the pattern. You could say it was tailor made.

The Allied Chemical Plant is a prominent resident of Baltimore's recently revived Inner Harbor; physically prominent but, until recently, not often noticed. Look east from the World Trade Center observation deck and the plant is center stage. Boaters head straight for it as they leave the harbor for the Bay. From Harbor Place the massive complex blends with the surrounding industrial structures. Its somber, dark color matches the tone of the steely water. Move closer, to the piers off Lancaster Street, and listen. It seems to breathe, as if the railroad cars grinding on their tracks, the low rumble of machinery and the shrill bells and buzzers are the sounds of a living being.

This snoring mammoth is most impressive in the early morning. The colors of dawn are a backdrop for its striking silhouette, black shapes against oranges and mauves. These images inspired the concept for the architectural graphics now enlivening the facade.

Allied Chemical's Baltimore operation is currently and historically significant. It is the only plant in the United States producing a full line of chromium based chemicals. With ore imported from Africa and Finland the plant produces primarily sodium bichromate dihydrate and chromic acid, as well as a range of related chemicals, for use in products as diverse as orange and yellow dyes, fertilizers and recording tapes. The manila envelope on your desk, for example, was most likely colored with a product from Allied.

In the early 1800's a Baltimorean, Isaac Tyson, discovered chromite ore on his estate. At first he exported the ore to European paint and ceramic factories. As additional chromite mines were discovered in Maryland and Pennsylvania his operation expanded to manufacturing. Tyson's company led the field in chemical technology. In the late 1800's local chromite deposits ran dry and he began importing ore from Turkey. His Fell's Point operation had no competitors until 1882 when several other plants were founded in the area.

In 1908 these smaller plants and Tyson's merged. Continually expanding, the Baltimore Works became the most technologically advanced in the group and eventually the other facilities were phased out. Today's complex was rebuilt in the 1950's and expanded in 1967. It has been a part of the Allied Chemical Corporation since 1954. Occupying one of the most prominent sites on the Inner Harbor, the plant is a stable, long term resident.

The idea of creating architectural graphics for Allied Chemical was developed by Charles Center Inner Harbor Management (a private, nonprofit land development corporation involved with the cities' interests) and the management of the Baltimore Works of the Allied Corporation. All were concerned with upgrading the visual character of the area and maintaining the company's reputation as a conscientious neighbor in the evolving Inner Harbor. In early 1983 Land Design/Research, Inc., was commissioned to study the situation and generate several concepts.

Midsummer the paint was ordered and meetings with the contractor were held. The procedure for painting a building of this scale and under such specific working conditions required careful planning. As does everyone inside the plant, designers and painters had to wear hard hats, goggles and respirators at all times and have a clean shaven face. The painters had to schedule their work around the operation of the plant, often using weekends to paint heavily used areas.

Work started at the top. The painting pattern was transferred to the building using a grid and spot measurements. The concept of following the roof contour usually required merely measuring the distance from any point on the roofline. But often the silhouette to be painted reflected structures set back from the roof edge, such as smokestacks. Many times a shape measured correctly would look wrong. Measurements then had to be visually approximated with trial and error adjustments.

To provide an ideal surface for the epoxy enamel paint the buildings were patched, bare metal was primed and smooth surfaces were acid-etched. The entire facade was then incrementally waterblasted to remove every trace of dirt. Pollution gathered on the surface so quickly that cleaning could not precede painting by more than a few days. Therefore, crews were organized for each task. The first group waterblasted the area to be painted. The design was chalked on by the next crew and the light gray was sprayed on. The third crew delineated the sharp edge between the light and medium grays with brushes. The next band was sprayed on and the darker areas were edged.

In most cases the roofs were not painted. The south face, however, was an exception. The roof is so low and large that it is more visible than others. On that inclined plane the width of the bands was increased so that they seem equal to the bands on adjoining vertical surfaces. The painting pattern for Allied was determined from one major point of view for each facade—directly in front, in true elevation. It is actually seen from many different angles, some of which render the pattern meaningless. The design is best seen in the process of moving past the building. Interpretation of the colored bands changes depending on where the viewer stands and whether or not he moves. The concept becomes obvious as each area is approached head on.

Cynthia L. Rienzo
Land Design/Research, Inc.

Perhaps the most striking effect is the interaction of paint, sky and water. The light gray is so similar to a typical Maryland sky that it tends to blend in. The darker gray matches the deep tone of the Bay water, creating the sinking illusion.

It is hoped that this new coat for Allied Chemical will be interesting and attractive, yet not intrusive. It is meant to be noticed in passing, then casually examined and considered with each successive viewing. Allied's intent is to advertise their character, not their product. The paint does not decorate, camoflage or disguise the industrial personality. It emphasized the grace and dignity of form. That form is a component of Baltimore's image; the image of a city at work.

2.

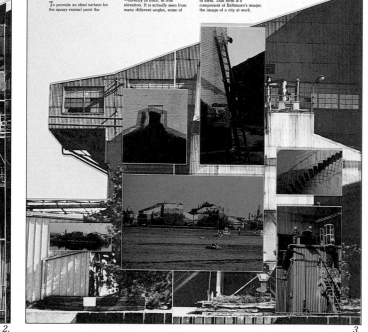

3.

4.

5.

6.

7.

8.

9.

preparation of presentation and working drawings, and on-site supervision, the designers also prepared a series of display boards to explain the concept and details of the whole process of design and implementation.

Client: Charles Center/Inner Harbor Management Corp., Baltimore; Allied Chemical Corp., Baltimore
Design firm: Land Design/Research, Inc., Columbia, MD
Designers: Cynthia L. Hanegraaf, project designer; Timothy Promen, designer; Robert Gorman, Patrick Mullaly, principals-in-charge

6, 7. *The banded gray solution was derived from sky and water colors.*
8. *Painting in progress.*
9. *The Allied plant with color-test panels as seen from Harborplace. Historic ship* Constellation *is in foreground.*

150 Alhambra Center

Unanimous praise by the *Casebook* jury for this office building exterior and parking garage signing commended particularly the elegant tubular steel clearance structures, and the way in which the tubular element has become the playful yet functional design theme of the entire system.

Montgomery Design was commissioned by the architects four months before the building was occupied, and given a stringent $13,750 design budget. The designers were required to produce a system that would underscore the presence of the new building in the city (Coral Gables, Florida), restrict the entry of over-sized vehicles to the parking garage, promote traffic flow through the parking areas and identify parking levels, and include compatible tenant signing, most especially a major entrance sign for the NCNB National Bank.

Detailed design development was based on a study of exposed beam and utility plans to ensure no obstruction of the signs by structural or mechanical elements. Several letter sizes were tried to assure legibility on the cylindrical form of the sign faces. The disc shapes for the two-dimensional signs and the use of dots in the specially designed arrow, as well as on the elevator cab signs, were derived from the cross section of the tubes, made prominent by the exposed joint details.

When design documents were almost complete, the construction budget was cut back radically to just $20,000 (excluding tenant signs). This involved the designers in a good deal of negotiation with

1.

2.

1, 2. Use of dots in main logo is derived from cross section of tubular steel clearance structures.

fabricators to come up with techniques and materials substitutions that would not affect the esthetic quality or durability of the signs. To meet strength requirements, steel tubes were specified for the exterior parking clearance structures, and steel was also used for the bank entry arch because in this application it proved less expensive than aluminum. A clear polyurethane finish was applied to these structures to give an added luster to the vibrant red and metallic silver colors.

The steel bank entry arch, with its base mounted within the building setback, projects out at the top to provide a source of illumination for the logotype mounted on the wall above.

Inside the garage, PVC tubes proved both cheaper and lighter than either steel or aluminum. In strategic locations, aluminum panels are curved to fit walls and columns. Red and silver is used for exterior, main floor and visitors' parking. A palette of orange, yellow, green, blue, violet and gray provides color coding for the different parking levels. Futura Medium is used throughout.

Client/Architect: Modular Architecture, Inc., Edgewater, FL
Design firm: Montgomery Design, Coconut Grove, FL
Designers: Margaret Montgomery, Maria Lopez, José Vicente, Ellie Stein, Adrian Lee, Elsa Lopez
Fabricator: 2001 Group

3, 4. *Arrow and numeral dots repeat cylindrical theme.*
5. *Drawing (front elevation) of proposed plaza sculpture, never implemented because of budget constraints.*
6. *Whimsical hand graphic system was also a casualty of budget cuts. But the designers painted one graphic on a wall themselves to insure its survival.*
7-10. *Discs, cylinders and curved monolith evidence a consistency in concept and execution.*

3.

4.

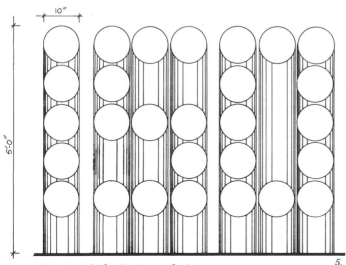

PLAZA SCULPTURE · FRONT ELEVATION

5.

REMEMBER PARK TWO 2

6.

7.

8.

9.

10.

The Home Club

The tools of home repair, dashingly painted on the exterior walls of a drab, concrete building, serve as both decoration and identification of a discount home improvement store in San Bernadino, California. An extremely limited budget, and even tighter schedule, telescoped the entire design-approval-fabrication process, and the painting was accomplished in little more than a week. Since city ordinances had greatly restricted permissible sign types and sizes, the building in effect became its own sign, with excellent results. The store quickly rose to be the highest-volume unit in the chain.

After studying site drawings and visiting the site, Hinsche & Associates developed two concepts—the other was a typographical solution—and presented them in model form to the developer. Once the scheme was approved, they refined it and took it straight into working drawings without further client review. They met with the painters, who then went ahead and painted, with minimal supervision from the design team. "We held our breath," says designer James Guerard, "because time restraints had precluded any testing of the impact of the design at actual scale."

The elements of home repair—a saw, a wrench, a paintbrush, a hammer, a faucet and a light bulb—literally cover the sides of the 30'-tall building, in shades of orange, red, green, blue and lilac. A few aluminum roof extensions were fabricated to allow the graphics to break out of this most banal of concrete boxes.

1.

2.

Client: The Sunset Group,
San Bernadino, CA
Design firm: Hinsche + Associates,
Santa Monica, CA
Designers: James Guerard, John Tom,
Gary Hinsche (president)

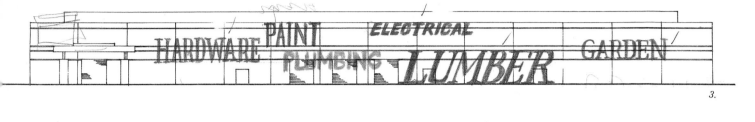

3.

4.

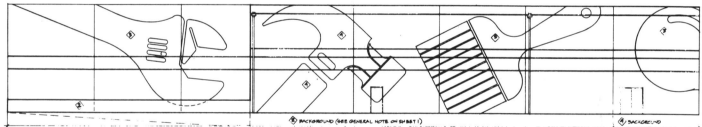

SOUTH ELEVATION

5.

NORTH ELEVATION

6.

1,2. "Before" and "after" photos show
transformation of a drab concrete
structure by means of bold, simple, and
appropriate painted graphic facade
treatment.
3, 4. Studies of alternative treatments.
5, 6. Elevational drawings showing
projection of hammer above roofline, on
north elevation.

7.

8.

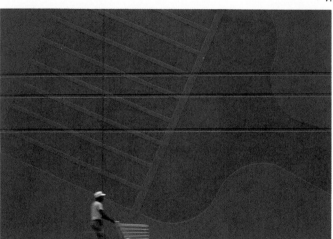

9.

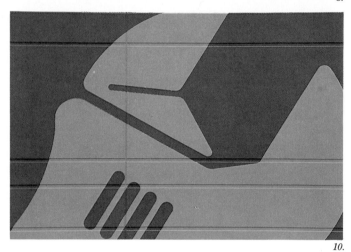

10.

7-11. *Components of home repair become effective wall supergraphics for home-improvement store. Some aluminum roof extensions were added to allow saw-handle and hammer to project beyond the building's roofline.*

11.

1.

Chaste, white surfaces with subtly-lit accent colors set the stage for an office signing system that forms a deft counterpoint to the architecture. Designed by architects Gensler and Associates for their own San Francisco headquarters, the system was intended to "play off the architectural elements of the design, which are angular and simple, and make its own strong statement based on the design of the space."

For the most important component, the main lobby sign, an aged Italianate Florentine finish was selected to provide a diverting contrast to the slick white walls on which the letters are mounted. But Helvetica Light, the corporate typeface, affirms the essentially modern context and message of the firm. The wooden letters were painted in three colors, then gold-leafed and distressed by hand, and finally left out in the elements to acquire the patina of age.

Considerable experiment was needed before the desired finish was achieved. It was also quite difficult to find a satisfactory way to make the letters adhere to the wall surface. In the end, the sign was secured by means of pins inserted through the face of each letter.

"The angle and bevel of the restroom signs," says designer John Bricker, "were designed to play off the angular and geometrical treatment of the space plan and interior design. The base color is the same as the white vinyl used on the walls, while the colors—gold, red and blue—complement accent colors used in the space. Italic lettering was specified to reinforce the angular concept."

Other signs, in Univers and Bodoni Italic, silkscreened directly on to the laminated wall surfaces, also use graphic motifs that play off the angular geometric themes. The stair sign denotes the edge of a hardware-free flush door by means of a vertical bar graphic that also indicates the door's swing to the user.

"Is it too trendy?" one *Casebook* juror wondered aloud. But the others found it engaging, understated and an effective communicator at several levels. The gilded letters were a surprising, but ingratiating, touch. The whole could perhaps be taken as a witty and good-humored comment on the architectural "pluralism" of today.

1. *Gilt lettering on a slick white wall is effective main lobby sign for a firm of architects.*

Client: Gensler and Associates/
Architects, San Francisco
Design firm: Gensler Graphics Group
Designers: John Bricker, Gail Gordon,
Orlando Diaz-Azcuy
Photographer: Toshi Yoshimi
Fabricator: Thomas Swan Signs

*2, 3. Helvetica Light lettering with an aged
Italianate finish playfullly suggests the
modern and historical themes that
characterize today's "architectural
pluralism."*
*4. Office environment is one of white
surfaces, subtle lighting and clear accent
colors.*
*5. Floor number and elevator code message
is silkscreened directly to laminate wall.*
*6. Stair sign silkscreened directly to plastic
laminate door uses bar graphic to indicate
door's edge and swing.*

2.

3.

4.

In Case Of
Fire Use Stairs
For Exit. Do Not
Use Elevator.

No Smoking
In Elevator.

5.

Stairs

6.

Louisiana World's Fair

Despite the severe contemporary criticism usually accorded them, world's fairs do have a way of expressing the design dogma of their eras—or lack of it—albeit in a contrived and self-conscious context. The 1892 Columbian Exposition in Chicago had its establishment Beaux Arts palaces by Charles Follen McKim, Richard Morris Hunt, and Charles B. Atwood, among others, but there was also one pioneering precursor of modernism in the transportation building by Louis Henry Sullivan. The 1964 New York World's Fair was an emporium of latter-day International Style pavilions. The 1984 Louisiana World's Fair in New Orleans was, by and large, a free-form assemblage of funky stage or film sets rendered in the pastel colors so beloved of the post-modernists. The design firm of Communication Arts was charged with the task of designing "an entertaining but

functional signing and site amenities" system that would help to make the fair intelligible as well as amusing to its visitors.

The historic warehouse district of New Orleans, alongside the Mississippi River, was renovated to provide fitting corporate pavilions and international exhibit spaces, and a permanent 300,000-sq. ft. Convention Center was erected for initial use at the fair. But according to R. Allen Eskew of the New Orleans firm of Perez Associates, architects for the fair, the spaces in between mattered more than the buildings in this instance, and the "soul" of the fair was really the Wonderwall, conceived with architects Charles Moore and William Turnbull, a 2400'-long, continuous float construction of filigree scaffolding, arrayed with a collage of papier-maché, styrofoam, fiberglass and sheet metal mermaids, river and sea monsters, flotsam and jetsam,

and enhanced by integrated theatrical lighting.

In such a context, the graphics and street furniture program assumed more than its ordinary importance, since it had to contribute to the festive, funky ambience, as well as provide visitors with the information and amenities they needed to take full advantage of all the fair had to offer.

Since water, or more specifically the "World of Rivers," was the central theme of the fair, the 80-acre site was divided into six water-related "neighborhoods," each one characterized by its own graphic symbol and color selection. Thus, the ocean district was represented by a blue and lavender wave against a foam-colored background, the river by a jumping fish in light blue against gray, the lake by orange boats on a purple ground, and the others—ice, snow and rain—by variations of the predominantly gray-blue-

turquoise-pink graphic color palette.

Components of the system included directories, thematic light poles, street signs, bollards and neighborhood gateways. Custom-designed trash receptacles and benches were jettisoned from the system because a strict $2-million construction budget demanded considerable pruning and tailoring of the original concept.

The candy store and the ice cream parlor—the delights of childhood parties—provided an additional source of imagery appropriate to the fairground. So the bollards were like candy canes, and the thematic light poles somehow contrived to combine the aura of ribbons and paper hats with a shellfish motif.

Because of their strength and bending characteristics, painted steel and aluminum were used for all tubular and structural elements, except the

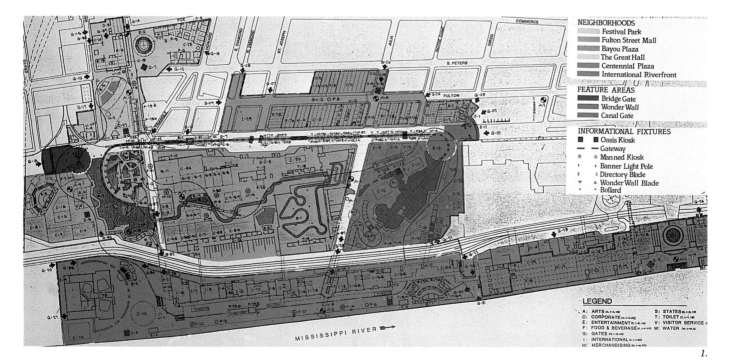

1.

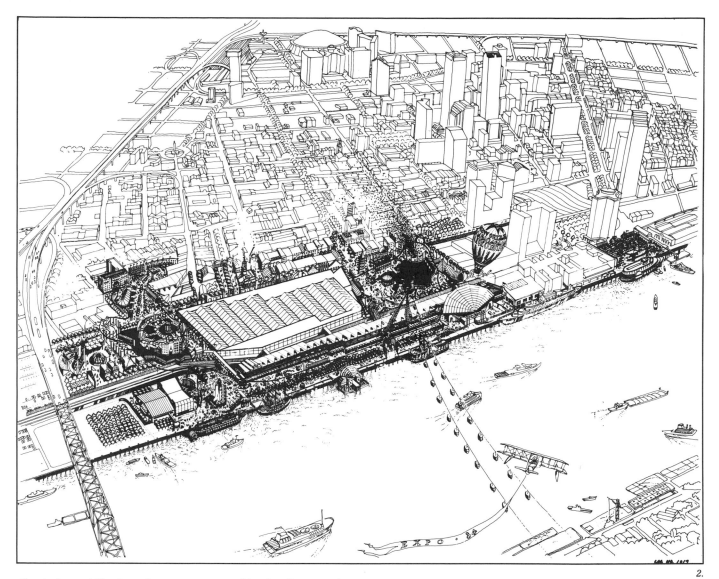

directories and illuminated portions of the light poles, where internal lighting requirements made heat-formed plastic a more appropriate material. Italia Medium, for its "legible, festive and international flavor," was specified for all directional and regulatory signing. One change

suggested by the client was the substitution of nautical pennants for the fan-shaped banners, initially proposed by Communication Arts as an integral part of the thematic light poles.

Careful site and circulation studies, with the pedestrian very much in mind, were the

basis for positioning and scaling of the components. Directories were 8' high, gateways and light poles 18', street signs 9'6", and bollards 7'. In certain locations, New Orleans site conditions made it necessary to use above-grade bases for the pole-mounted elements.

Client: Louisiana World Exposition
Design firm: Communication Arts, Inc., Boulder, CO
Designers: Richard Foy, Michael Gericke, art directors; Donna Hoover, Chi-ming Kan, Susie Kinzig, Patrick VanHook, designers
Architect: Perez Associates, New Orleans (R. Allen Eskew, lead architect), with Charles Moore and William Turnbull, Los Angeles
Consultant: Richard Peters, fair lighting
Fabricators: Young Electric Sign Co.; Gillman Paint Co.

1. Site plan of fair shows color-coded "neighborhoods."
2. Fanciful perspective of fairground points up importance of the spaces between buildings.

Photo by © Alan Karchmer

3. *Study model (¼-size) of lightpoles with aluminum streamers.*

4. *Full-size prototype with a "neighborhood" color applied to hand-bent lightpole streamers.*

5. *Actual lightstandards with pennant banners and streamers attached. Wonderwall alligators in background.*

6. *Monorail stations are color-coded for neighborhood orientation.*

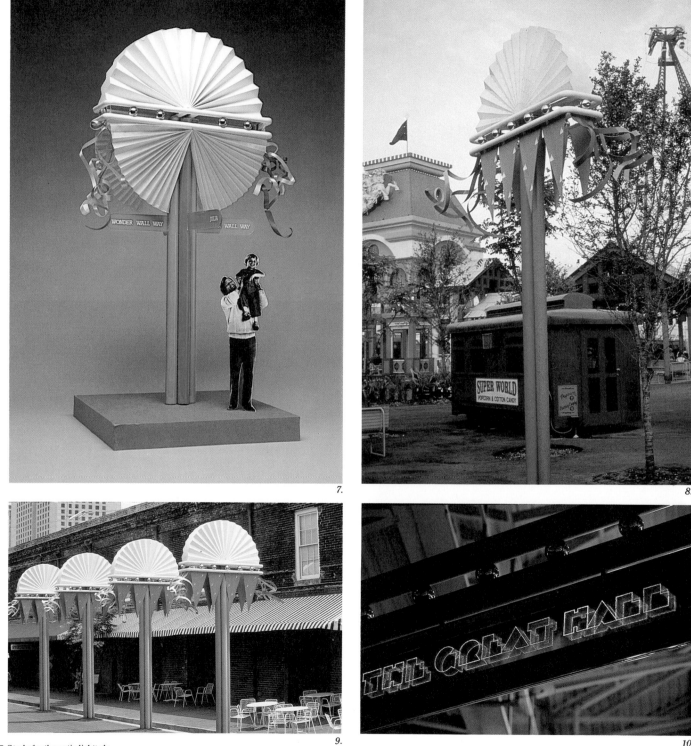

7. Study for thematic lightpole.
8, 9. Actual lightpoles in position and color-
coded to fairground "neighborhoods."
10. Fiber-optic lighting for "neighborhood"
gateway identifying sign.

11.

12.

13.

14.

11. Six-foot-high bollards define a special area.
12. Detail of bollard.
13. Color-coded street sign.
14. Each "neighborhood" had gateway with fiber-optic lighting.

U.S. Fidelity and Guarantee Corporate Headquarters

A corporate headquarters—including an advanced, 140,000-sq. ft. data-processing center—on a historic site in a park-like setting near Baltimore, demanded not only architectural sensitivity, but a certain graphic élan to tie the disparate units together and provide an internal logic for each department.

As architects for the entire 350,000-sq. ft. development, RTKL was able to use its own graphic designers, and this of course gave them a head start in integrating the signing with the site planning and architecture. However, the decision to extend RTKL's graphic responsibility to the interior came much later, allowing the design team only six months to work out and complete a very complex assignment.

This is surely the first time the *Print Casebooks* have ever included building identification signing inspired by a lapel pin! But such was indeed the case at USF&G, whose Facilities vice-president, Michael Casey, was prone to wear a neat, USF&G-enamelled lapel pin at meetings with his architects. Translated, the pin's motif became a palette of gold leaf, deep blue and burgundy identifying signs, appearing sometimes in plaque form, sometimes as gilt-edged low wood monoliths, and sometimes as gilt letters applied directly to an exterior wall. Directional signing followed a similar pattern, except that white reflective lettering was used to replace the gold, in the interests of better night-time visibility. Inside, the same sign profile was maintained, but scale, color and materials changed to complement interior finishes. Essentially, the USF&G interior signing consists of ¼" bevelled acrylic face plates with applied, painted or screened lettering, half-round brushed aluminum top and bottom trim, and a palette of gray or beige background colors in harmony with the prevailing interior décor.

But the most inventive part of the program, and the one that led the jury to unanimously include it in the *Casebook*, was the signing for the vast Data Processing Center. They felt the graphics here had become an important environmental element, doing much to enliven what must inevitably be a repetitive and highly functional workplace.

Within the Data Processing Center, 24 different illuminated graphic assemblages are hung at the intersection of cross corridors or "streets" with the main circulation route through the department. Each of these assemblages is tied in to employee directories at the ends of each "street," which in turn tie in to the employee name plaques at each work station. Each of these special overhead graphic assemblies carries a capital letter, and then as an aid to identity and orientation, the name of a city or county in Maryland beginning with that letter, and a tinted engraving illustrating something characteristic of the place so named. The signs are arranged alphabetically to make navigation as easy as possible, and the capital letters are large enough to be read from the far ends of the corridors.

To create this effect, each assembly consists of four 2' by

1.

2.

1. *Aerial view of headquarters complex. Signing program had to integrate modern and historic structures.*
2. *Gilt-edged wood monolith uses color palette of royal blue and burgundy, derived from a vice-president's enameled lapel pin.*

1'6" clear acrylic panels hung in front of each other. On the first is screened the place name; on the second appears the initial letter; on the third, the illustration; and on the fourth, the place name again appears for viewing from the opposite direction. Each panel is edge-lit from above so that the silk-screened portions catch the light and glow.

Garamond Book Italic was used on all interior signing; Garamond Book Roman on the exterior signs.

Client: U.S. Fidelity and Guarantee Co., Baltimore
Design firm: RTKL Associates Inc., Baltimore
Designers: Ann Dudrow, Nicole Pillorgé
Architect: RTKL Associates, Inc.
Consultant: ISD (interior design)
Fabricators: Federal Sign; Belsinger Sign Works; Globe Silk Screen

3.

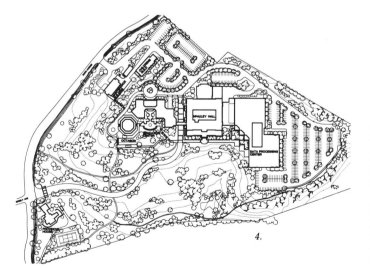

4.

5.

6.

7.

8.

9.

3, 6-9. Acrylic panel signs hung at "street"
intersections in large data center identify
and orient by means of place-name motifs.
4. Site plan shows relative size of data
processing center.
5. Each place-named section in data center
has its own employee directory to tie in
with "street" signs.

The 1985 contract design market at the Dallas World Trade Center was informed and kept up to the mark by the ubiquitous catchword "InfoWorks," which made its appearance in a number of guises—on banners, on posters, on shopping bags, programs, booklets, signs, ads and displays. An abbreviation of the slogan "Information that Works: Design, Technology, Productivity," "InfoWorks" was intended to set the upbeat tone of the market and stimulate the furniture manufacturers and the interior designers and architects, who specify their products, to enter into a productive level of communication.

Designer Woody Pirtle's symbol subtly combined the three component themes. The brush stroke symbolized art and design; the pixelated pattern, contemporary technology; and the ascending steps of the bar graph, productivity. But there was something lighthearted about the symbol's application— the whisk of a paintbrush across a banner or a pamphlet— something to be enjoyed, but not perhaps taken too seriously as propaganda. The clear primary color scheme tended to reinforce this impression. Red, blue, yellow, black and white— boldly applied—were calculated to jolt any conventioneer out of boredom or complacency.

The chief environmental graphic element was the series of fourteen 16′ banners hung between the 5th and 6th floors in the open atrium of the Grand Hall of the Trade Center to call attention to the concentration of showroom activity on these floors. To marry the modern

and classical sources of contemporary design, Helvetica Bold and Bodoni type were used in combination on all components.

1. Conference symbol combined three themes—art, technology and productivity.
2. Banners were hung in Dallas World Trade Center atrium to identify floors on which chief conference activities were taking place.
3. Details of conference program.

Client: Trammel Crow Co., Dallas
Design firm: Pirtle Design, Dallas
Designers: Woody Pirtle, Mike Schroeder, Jeff Wiethman
Fabricators: Fox Signs, Heritage Press
Consultant: O'Malley & Co. Ltd.

2.

3.

4.

5.

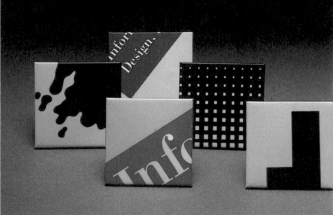

6.

7.

4. Banners in atrium were a colorful
conference announcement and a dramatic
counterpoint to the architecture.
5-7. Graphics program embraced everything
from banners and posters to displays,
packages, samples, notions and shopping
bags.

Environmental Graphics/96